PERFECT PRESERVES

PERFECT PRESERVES
Provisions from the Kitchen Garden

NORA CAREY

PHOTOGRAPHS BY MICK HALES

STEWART, TABORI & CHANG
New York

Text copyright © 1990 Nora Carey
Photographs copyright © 1990 Mick Hales
Published in 1990 by
Stewart, Tabori & Chang, Inc.
575 Broadway, New York, New York 10012

Library of Congress Cataloging-in-Publication Data
Carey, Nora.
    Perfect preserves/Nora Carey: photographs by Mick Hales.
      p. cm.
    Includes bibliographical references.
    ISBN 1-55670-132-2
      1. Food—Preservation.   I. Hales, Michael.   II. Title.
TX601.C345   1990
641.4—dc20   89-28585
                                                    CIP

Distributed in the U.S. by Workman Publishing, 708 Broadway, New York, New York 10003
Distributed in Canada by Canadian Manda Group, P.O. Box 920 Station U. Toronto, Ontario M8Z 5P9
Distributed in all other territories by Little, Brown and Company, International Division, 34 Beacon Street, Boston, Massachusetts 02108

Below: Rows of apple trees at Hope End, Ledbury, Herefordshire. Overleaf: The kitchen garden at Clapham House, Litlington, Sussex. Pages 10–11: Windfall apples and early-season pumpkins at Clapham House.

Printed in Japan
10 9 8 7 6 5 4 3 2 1

CONTENTS

In memory of A.M.L.C.

1925–1965

INTRODUCTION

Preserving food was not an inherent part of my childhood. Although my mother was a wonderful cook, and undoubtedly the catalyst for my eventual interest in food, preserving the seasons in a bottle was something she did not expose me to. I suspect that in the sixties preserving was considered an old-fashioned thing to do if you lived in a suburban American community. During summer vacations on Cape Cod, I used to observe my uncle while he made beach plum jelly, real cranberry juice, and rose hip jam. The process seemed magical but incomprehensible. The progression from the raw fruit stage to pans of boiling, sputtering fruit, to jelly bags, and then jars of crystal clear jelly was mystifying. Many years later I had the opportunity to do intensive research on the subject and discovered the logic behind the techniques.

Fresh from a year at La Varenne in Paris, I moved to London to be a researcher for Time-Life Books. I was assigned the preserving volume of the Good-Cook series, which turned out to be a fortuitous appointment, and as a result preserving became an exciting extension to my culinary training.

When I returned to France with my newly educated eye, all the available commercial preserves took on a different dimension. I no longer cast a casual glance over preserves but looked to them for inspiration for my own trials and experimentations.

I was fascinated by the appearance and contents of every jar I saw, whether in a neighborhood market or in one of the more prestigious food shops in Paris. Trips to the Madeleine and the Opéra areas were always extended by visits to Fauchon, Hédiard, Paul Courcellet, and Tanrade. Fauchon always displays amazingly large bottles of whole preserved fruit, prepared vegetables neatly arranged, and complete regional dishes like *coq au vin* and *pot-au-feu*. Hédiard is the temple for sweet tooths—famous for its *pâtes de fruits*, or fruit pastes, and a vast range of bottled fruit syrups and purées. For flavored vinegars and interesting jams, Paul Courcellet is a good stop.

Tanrade was for years the ultimate shop for jams and jellies. The Art Deco building on Rue Vignon was truly a masterpiece of design. Every detail was conceived with the fabrication of jams and jellies in mind. I was particularly amused by the wrought-iron chandeliers that incorporated the forms of jam jars within their structure. At Tanrade you could gauge the seasons by the stock of goods. Soft-fruit jams in early summer and quince, pear, and even medlar jams in autumn. Sadly, this family-run business came to a halt in the late eighties since the owners were getting on in age and the younger generations pursued other interests.

My time in France has clearly had an influence on my approach to preserving, but trips to Italy and back to England and America always provide fresh ideas. The English kitchen gardens, both formal and cottage-scale ones, have been a particular influence and obvious source of inspiration for this book. But no matter where you live, the fundamental rules of preserving should be defined by the quality and seasonal availability of the raw materials. Despite the wide use of air-freighting and exchange of fresh produce between countries, preserving should be about treating locally grown produce. Preserves made with produce within hours of being picked off the vine or unearthed from the soil will always be superior to those made with tired fruits and vegetables. Always remember that preserving does not improve the basic quality of the raw goods; it only maintains it.

If you are fortunate enough to have the space and the inclinition for gardening, select seeds, bushes, and trees with preserving in mind. Varieties of fruits and vegetables will vary from region to region, and there are always some that are better suited for preserving. Experimentation in this area

Freshly gathered rose hips for making syrups and jellies.

BOTTLING

Until the technological advances of deep-freezing became widespread, bottling or canning was the most frequently used method for preserving fruits, vegetables, meat, and fish in North America and Europe. Technically, bottling and canning refer to two different processes. The terms are often used interchangeably, however, because their principles are similar. In both cases the food is heated in order to kill harmful organisms and create a seal to prevent the entry of additional bacteria. In bottling, the process is carried out in glass jars; in canning, it occurs in metal cans. The temperature required to efficiently preserve a given food is determined by the density of the food, its level of acidity, its temperature when put in the container, and the capacity of the container.

Of all the variables, acidity is the most important consideration. High-acid fruits and some vegetables, like tomatoes, require a temperature of only between 165° F. and 212° F. (74° C. and 100° C.) to kill yeasts, molds, and bacteria that would otherwise contribute to rot and decay. In low-acid foods—most vegetables, meats, fish, and poultry—a higher temperature is required to kill spoiler organisms. Since these higher temperatures can only be achieved in special pressure canners, this process is best left to industrial services. The greatest threat to low-acid bottled or canned foods is the bacteria *Clostridium botulinum* (which produces the deadly toxin that causes botulism), because it thrives in an airtight environment. Fortunately the bacteria cannot survive in an acidic environment, thus making high-acid fruits safe to bottle or can.

The two terms most commonly associated with bottling are "hot pack" and "cold pack." In the hot-pack method, cooked fruit, such as Whole Apricots in Vanilla Syrup (page 69), is packed into a warm preserving jar with a hot liquid and processed in a hot water bath. Confusion about this term arises when the process is used for cold or raw food. But raw food can also be covered with a hot liquid and processed by the hot-pack method. For the cold-pack method, all elements start off cold: Uncooked food is packed in jars, covered with a cold liquid, and the jars are placed in a cold water bath, which is then brought to a boil to begin sterilization.

The best containers to use are special glass jars or bottles. There are two standard kinds: jars with clamp lids and rubber gaskets and jars with screw-band lids and separate flat metal lids. The jars can be used repeatedly, but the rubber gaskets and flat lids must be replaced with new ones once the seals have been broken. Do not recycle mayonnaise, peanut butter, or mustard jars, as the screw-band lid may be weakened and the glass may not be tempered to withstand the boiling water in a water bath.

Concerning sterilization, it is not necessary to sterilize jars before filling them with food to be preserved if they are to be processed in a water bath, as the jars will be sterilized during the processing time. All jars should be simply scrubbed clean with hot sudsy water, rinsed well, and dried before packing.

The raw or cooked fruit should be packed comfortably into the containers. Do not overpack, because the food will expand slightly during the processing. The liquid added to the jar should only come to the capacity level marked on it. This allows for a "headspace" of at least ½ inch, which will permit expansion of the food and boiling of the liquid. If the jars are filled beyond the capacity mark, the excess volume may prevent a seal from forming.

Fruit can be layered with sugar and processed, but experience has shown me that a sugar syrup gives better results. The syrup can vary in sugar concentration (see Simple Sugar Syrups, page 235) and can be prepared with water, fruit juice, wine, or a combination of liquids.

Once the food is packed into the clean jars or bottles, the procedures for hot- or cold-pack preserving are similar. The containers are lowered either into a special "canner" fitted with racks and clips to keep the containers in place or into a large deep stockpot or similar pan. With a stockpot a few precautions must be taken to protect the jars from cracking. A wire rack must be placed on the bottom of the pot to keep the jars from direct contact with the heat, and each bottle should be wrapped in cloth or newspaper to prevent their rattling around.

Once the jars are secure in the canner or stockpot, the container is filled with enough water (hot or cold depending on the processing method) to cover the tops of the jars by at least one inch. It is important that there be ample headspace between the water level and the top of the pan to allow the water to boil without spilling over. The water is then slowly brought to the necessary sterilization temperature—which can range from 169° F. to 212° F. (76° C. to 100° C.), depending on the acidity and density of the food—and maintained for the required time. Canners are equipped with a thermometer that fits into the lid. If no canner or thermometer is available, fruits, acidic vegetables, and low-sugar preserves can be processed in boiling water to eliminate the guesswork.

In this book, individual recipes indicate the most appropriate processing times, which are calculated from the moment the boiling point is reached. Once the preserves have been processed for the required time, leave the jars in the water until they are cool enough to be handled safely. Jars in a canner will lift out neatly from a central supporting system. If the jars have been processed in a stockpot, lift each one individually with long tongs. Leave the jars on a work surface overnight or until completely cool. During the cooling process, the air will be forced out of the jars and seals will form.

Before storing, test the seal on each jar.

For screw-band jars, remove the outer ring and check that the remaining covering disk is concave. You should be able to pick up the jar by the disk if a seal has formed. For clamped or hinged jars with a rubber gasket, unhinge the clamp and hold the jar up by the glass lid. If in either case the seal has not been obtained, chill the food and consume it within a few days.

Store all bottled preserves in a cool, dark area for no more than one year. Although preserves on display may be attractive, the contents are light- and heat-sensitive and can deteriorate if not properly stored.

To break the seal on a screw-band jar, pry the flat lid off with the tip of a dull knife. For a clamp jar, give a strong tug on the protruding rubber portion of the gasket. If the contents of any jar smell suspicious, discard it. Do not taste.

SALTING AND PICKLING

SALTING

Salting is associated with primitive methods for prolonging the storage of food, and as a result it does not always enjoy a high profile when the options for preserving are under consideration. What needs to be appreciated in order to upgrade this unpopular image is that salt can transform certain raw ingredients into perfectly delightful, yet different, products. One-hundred-year-old salted eggs and six-month-old salted green beans are not to everyone's liking. However, such classic items as cured olives and sauerkraut would not exist without salt.

Salt preserves food by creating an environment wherein microorganisms are deprived of the moisture they require to survive. The salt can be applied dry or in brine. In dry-salting, the salt is rubbed directly onto a food's surface and in due course draws out the moisture and creates its own brine. The food reabsorbs the brine and is then "cured." This technique is best for small, flat foods that can readily absorb the salt. Among vegetables, shredded cabbage responds best to this treatment, but sliced turnips, carrots, and cucumbers also make interesting short-term preserves.

In brining, a food is immersed in a saline solution. As with the dry-salting method, the brine penetrates the cell structure of the food, replacing its natural moisture. Bacteria cannot survive in a 25-percent salt solution; the activity of most spoilage organisms is arrested in a 10-percent solution.

For both dry-salting and brining, only pure sea salt is recommended. Free-flowing or iodized salts contain chemicals that can interrupt the preserving process and even darken the food. And in addition, the impurities will cloud the liquid in a brine.

Concerning water for brines, stick to pure bottled water to avoid impurities and prevent clouding. This may seem an extravagant approach, but it is a small expense in view of the ingredients, labor, and time involved in making perfect preserves.

Equipment for brining should be non-porous and non-metallic. Glass and glazed stoneware are the most suitable. The equipment need not be sterilized but should be clean, well rinsed, and dry before it is used.

Dry-salting and brining should be carried out in a cool environment; a constant temperature between 68° F. and 72° F. (20° C. and 22° C.) is ideal. If the temperature is above or below this range, the process may be hampered.

Once the curing process is accomplished, all preserves should be stored in a cool place (60° F./16° C. or below). Shelf life varies according to the ingredients and has been indicated in this book when appropriate.

PICKLING

Pickling is a form of preserving food that is often coupled with salting, although the significant preserving agent is the acetic acid in vinegar, not salt. Vegetables and, to a lesser extent, fruits are first treated by dry-salting or brining to extract excess moisture and then immersed in a bath of vinegar. The vinegar replaces the moisture in the food and prohibits the growth of harmful microorganisms.

In order for the vinegar to be effective in its preserving roles, the level of acetic acid needs to be between 4 and 6 percent. Most commercial vinegars have the necessary acetic acid concentration. Homemade vinegars may also be used; however, check the level of acidity with a piece of litmus paper, available from a pharmacy. To increase the concentration of a vinegar boil it until the desired strength is attained.

The choice of vinegar to be used should be based on the marriage of flavors with the food to be preserved and in some cases the color. For example, pearl onions look amazing in red-wine vinegar, yet have a dull image in brown malt vinegar.

Wine vinegar: Wine vinegars result from the fermentation of red or white wine. The French word *vinaigre* is literally "sour wine." Wine vinegar is recommended for its smooth and subtle flavors.

Cider vinegar: Cider vinegar is made from fermented apple juice and as a result has a very fruity flavor. The best recommended use is with fruit-based chutneys.

Malt vinegar: Malt vinegar, a grain-based vinegar made from malted barley, has a very pronounced flavor and is not suitable for making subtle preserves.

Distilled vinegar: This vinegar is made by distilling malt vinegar, and as a result it becomes colorless. The distilling process also mellows the sharp pronounced flavors of the malt vinegar. Distilled vinegar is recommended when the color of the food itself is to be highlighted.

Another category of pickled fruits and vegetables includes those that are submerged in oil, rather than vinegar, for the final treatment. Vinegar plays a supporting role here, as salt does for vinegar-based pickles. The food is first blanched or cooked in vinegar, which replaces the natural moisture. Once drained, it is protected from harmful airborne organisms by submersion in oil. This technique is particularly good with artichokes (see Marinated Artichokes in Olive Oil, on page 167), which are served accompanied with some of the vinegar and oil sauce.

When preparing fruits and vegetables for pickling, remember that salt and vinegar together are corrosive. With the exception of stainless steel, never use metals when preparing these preserves. Storage containers should be made of glass or glazed stoneware. Do not use metal lids that will corrode from contact with the vinegar itself or the vapors. Glass jars with clamps and glass lids and plastic-lined screw caps are necessary. Paraffin sealing (see "Special Packaging and Labeling," page 52) is also a good choice for chutneys. The paraffin keeps out all air and eliminates the risk of evaporation and shrinkage.

All pickles should be stored in a cool, dark place. Most vinegar-based preserves require at least three months to mature, and are good for up to one year. Oil-based pickles keep for between three and six months, depending on the ingredients. Storage guidelines have been given for each pickle recipe in this book.

A private collection of herb-flavored vinegars on the mantle at Wiltshire Tracklements. Overleaf: a sampling of homemade preserves for the guests at Hunstrete House Hotel, Avon.

BLACK & RED CURRANT
CONSERVE
JULY '88

PEAR CHUTNEY
JULY '88

GRAPEFRUIT
MARM.
JULY '88

CHATEAU DU N
POUILLY SUR LO

SWEETENING

When thoughts are focused on preserving, the products that first spring to mind are those that depend on a sweetener as the preserving agent. The concept of preserving by sweetening is very elementary: When a high concentration of cane sugar, or similar ingredient, is combined with fresh food, the natural moisture of the food is saturated by the sweetener and the development and growth of harmful microorganisms are inhibited. Though fruits are the obvious subjects of this treatment, such vegetables as pumpkins and carrots make interesting sweet preserves.

The most commonly used sweetener for preserving is white cane sugar, but brown sugar, molasses, honey, and maple syrup can be substituted in varying proportions depending upon the preserve. The range of foods that can be preserved with a sweetener falls into very specific categories:

Jellies are clear, set gels made from strained fruit juices.

Jams/preserves are made from whole or sliced fruits. They should be soft enough to spread, but not runny.

Marmalades are clear jellies in which shreds of fruit have been suspended. By tradition, marmalades are usually made with citrus fruits, with shreds of peel suspended in the jelly.

Conserves are fruit mixtures, generally containing a citrus fruit, with dried fruits and nuts. Conserves are not set and are often called spoon sweets—that is, they can be eaten directly from the spoon.

Fruit curds are smooth spreads made from acidic fruits such as lemons, limes, and passion fruits with the inclusion of sugar, butter, and eggs.

Fruit butters are smooth spreads, similar to fruit curds, made with only fruit and sugar.

Fruit pastes and cheeses are similar to fruit butters but contain more sugar and are much thicker. Fruit pastes are usually presented in thin rolls or small squares. Fruit cheeses are often set in decorative molds (see Molded Peach "Cheese" on page 134).

Sugar is essential not only for preserving the fruit but, in such cases as jams and jellies, setting the product.

In general, half to equal weights of sugar to fruit will be sufficient. Less sugar can be used for preserves that don't need to set, but they should be processed briefly in a boiling water bath to prevent spoilage.

The skin, seeds, flesh, and cores of fruit contain pectose in varying amounts, which is converted to pectin when subjected to heat. Any fruit mixture will set providing that the quantities of pectin, sugar, and acid are adequate. Fruits that are particularly high in pectose and have medium to high levels of acid are apples, cranberries, currants, gooseberries, plums, quinces, and citrus fruits. Fruits low in pectose and acid include strawberries, rhubarb, and pears. Low-pectin fruits can benefit from the addition of a little lemon juice to boost the acidity and aid setting, or they can be combined with a high-pectin fruit.

TESTING THE PECTIN LEVEL

The amount of pectin present in a fruit juice can be measured approximately by combining 1 teaspoon juice with 2 tablespoons methylated spirits in a small bowl and swirling the mixture together for a few minutes, or until clotting develops. A large clot will indicate a high pectin level; a few small clots indicate a medium level; and scattered small beads indicate a low level. If the pectin level is medium or low, continue reducing the liquid until a large clot forms. *Discard the contents of the bowl and wash it in boiling water: methylated spirits are poisonous.*

Before embarking on any preserving project be sure that the fruits are well selected. Slightly under-ripe fruit is a little higher in pectose than mature or over-ripe fruit.

Slightly over-ripe fruit can be used for fruit butters and pastes, which rely more on reduction for a firm product rather than on pectin.

EQUIPMENT

The most important piece of equipment for making preserves in the jam and jelly family is a solid preserving pan. There are many debates over the choice of copper versus aluminum as regards the distribution of heat and retention of flavor and vitamins. I maintain that an old-fashioned unlined copper pan is the most efficient and admittedly the most aesthetically pleasing to use. The copper distributes the heat quickly and uniformly and in some cases enhances the color of the fruit. The only precaution with a copper preserving pan is to ensure that the interior is thoroughly cleaned before using. Any preserving pan should be shallow with a wide surface to facillitate evaporation thus reducing cooking time. Always make preserves in small batches; large batches of fruit require more cooking time and risk loss of flavor; also the setting ability of the pectin may diminish.

A kitchen scale is useful for weighing fruits and sugar. The relationship of the ingredients is easier to determine by weight than by volume.

During the cooking period of any fruit preserve, the impurities from the ingredients, including the sugar, will surface in a foamy sea. Skim the impurities off with a metal spoon. The main nuisance of the impurities is that, if left, they add a cloudy look to the preserve.

A thermometer is useful in gauging the jellying point of jams, jellies, and marmalades. In principle, a temperature of 220° F. (105° C.) indicates a jellying point. If a thermometer is unavailable, the thickness of the mixture should indicate doneness. As a test, place a tablespoon of the preserve on a cold plate and chill it for a few minutes. The jellying point has been reached if the mixture is firm enough to remain divided

Using a jelly bag (supported by the legs of an upside-down stool) to extract juice from cooked fruit.

when a finger is pushed through the center. If the mixture is not set, continue cooking it a little longer.

For jellies, a specially devised cheesecloth bag, called a jelly bag, should be used to separate the pulp from the fruit juice to be jellied. The cloth should always be dampened first so that it is less likely to absorb liquid from the fruit. The bag can be fastened to an upside-down stool (see photo above) with a bowl underneath to collect the juice. Once the contents of the preserving pan are tipped into the bag, allow the mixture to drain overnight. Do not press on the solids; any pulp will make the liquid cloudy.

A wide-neck funnel makes the task of transferring preserves into storage jars much more manageable. All storage jars should be heat-resistant. Sterilize all containers and any lids in a boiling water bath for 10 minutes and then drain upside down on a clean tea towel. Keep the jars warm until they are filled so they won't crack when the hot preserve is poured into them. Be certain that the containers are completely dry. Any moisture could result in mold.

Seal jars with either spring-clamp covers or twist-on lids while the preserve is either very hot or completely cooled. Condensation builds up with temperatures in between the extremes and can result in spoilage. Waxed disks and paraffin seals can also be used (see Special Packaging and Labeling, page 52).

Store all sweet preserves no longer than 1 year for best results. Keep the containers in a cool, dark place.

POTENTIAL PROBLEMS

Unset jams and jellies: If the mixture remains liquid after the recommended cooking period, add a proportionate amount of Apple Pectin Stock (page 63)—½ cup of stock for every 2 to 3 cups liquid—and continue to cook until the jellying point is reached.

Crystallized preserves: This indicates a deficiency in acid, which can sometimes be remedied by reheating the mixture with a little lemon juice—approximately 1 tablespoon for every 1 cup of preserve.

Mold: This is generally caused by inadequate sealing. If mold is detected, neatly scrape it off with a spoon and cover the surface with paraffin (see Special Packaging and Labeling, page 52).

Fermentation: This is an indication of insufficient cooking. There is no remedy for this; it is best to discard the goods.

Belle de Boskoop apple trees.

DOUSING IN ALCOHOL

Alcohol is an effective preserving agent. It is usually paired with soft fruits, transforming them into succulent alcohol-drenched morsels. Dousing any fruit in alcohol preserves it as a result of an exchange of liquids. The alcohol must be in sufficient strength and quantity to penetrate the cell structure of the fruit, replacing the water and killing microorganisms. Any spirit that is at least 40 percent alcohol (80 proof) will be effective. Wine, beer, and fortified wines such as Sherry and Port are not strong enough to kill spoilage organisms.

When deciding upon the spirit, keep in mind that the fruit and alcohol should make a happy marriage. With the right combination, the flavor exchange makes the resulting alcohol alone worth the exercise. This is particularly the case of Crème de Cassis (page 99) and Sloe Gin (page 149), in which recipes the fruit is discarded and the alcohol bottled separately once the berries have surrendered their juices. Brandy teams up best with the warm tastes of apricots; prunes are delicious with Armagnac; and cherries are ideal for a neutral-tasting *eau-de-vie*.

Sugar plays a supportive role when one preserves with alcohol, because it counteracts the tendency of alcohol to toughen and shrink fruit. In general, ½ cup sugar is a good balance for every pound of fruit and 2 cups spirits. The sugar can be added to the fruit in either dry or syrup form. The easiest method is simply to layer the fruit and sugar in a preserving jar with the alcohol. The jar will have to be rotated over a period of a few days to ensure that all the sugar is dissolved. If you make a sugar syrup with a few tablespoons water and the alcohol, the rotating process is not necessary.

As for equipment, all containers should have a tight-sealing lid to prevent the alcohol from evaporating. The containers do not have to be sterilized before filling; a good wash in hot sudsy water and a thorough drying are sufficient. Bottles that are corked can be dipped in sealing wax for an attractive finish.

All alcohol-doused preserves should be stored in dry, dark, cool conditions. A minimum storage period of one month is necessary to allow the alcohol and fruit to mature. However, most fruits, particularly prunes, improve with age, and it is therefore recommended to treasure your preserves over a few years and treat them as a vintage wine.

Once the containers have been opened, be sure the contents are always covered with a liquid. If the fruit or alcohol is not as sweet as you may prefer, Simple Sugar Syrup (page 235) can be added.

A corner of the greenhouse at Clapham House is used for storing garden tools.

DEEP-FREEZING

Of all the preserving techniques, deep-freezing is perhaps the most commonly used method for prolonging the life of a food. Its popularity is probably due to its simplicity. In addition, unlike other preserving techniques, which actually transform the food into another guise, freezing barely alters the flavor of fruits and vegetables. If foods are handled properly, freezing is also considered to be the best method for preserving nutritional value.

The principles of freezing are very basic. The extreme cold inhibits the activity of enzymes that induce changes in color, flavor, and texture in foods. Enzyme activity cannot be completely arrested, however, and so foods will still deteriorate in the freezer over an extended period of time. In general, most fruits and vegetables will remain in good condition for up to one year in a deep-freezer.

By definition, a deep-freezer should operate at a temperature of 0° F. ($-18°$ C.) or below. Any food introduced to a freezer of this temperature will quickly adapt and achieve a solid state. The rapid drop in temperature is critical in preserving the quality of the product. Fast-freezing converts the water in the food to small ice crystals, whereas slow-freezing produces large crystals. During the storage periods, the crystals expand and can ruin the cell structure of the food, which in turn affects the flavor and texture. Small crystals are thus considered to be less damaging than larger ones.

When selecting fruits and vegetables for the freezer, keep in mind that the quality of the food that emerges from the freezer will only be as good as the quality that went in. Freezing maintains the quality of a food but does not enhance it.

As for all preserving techniques, it is essential that the fruits and vegetables be in prime condition and, ideally, that they be frozen within hours of being harvested. They should, of course, first be treated as if for immediate consumption. Sort through the food to discard any blemished or bruised specimens. Most fruits and vegetables should be washed and dried to eliminate dust or residual pesticides; the exception is berries, which tend to collapse when subjected to water.

Once sorted and washed, the food is then cut into convenient sizes or left whole before proceeding with freezing techniques. Fruits can be frozen either raw or cooked, and in one of three ways: in a dry pack, with sugar, or with a sugar syrup. Vegetables are best if blanched before freezing.

The method of freezing fruit depends on the nature of the raw ingredients and the intended use. Small fruits that do not require peeling and pitting—such as currants, raspberries, blackberries, gooseberries, blueberries, and grapes—can be frozen without sugar by the dry-pack method. The fruit should be spread out on trays so they do not touch each other and then quickly frozen for a couple of hours, or until solid. Quickly pack the fruit into freezer bags, eliminate as much excess air as possible, and seal.

Fruits that tend to discolor or have to be sliced to remove pits should be treated, before freezing, with sugar, which retards enzyme activity and preserves color. Although fruit can be simply tossed with granulated sugar and frozen, I find that the result resembles a sauce more than whole fruit; this can, however, be acceptable for some desserts and ice-cream toppings. As a rough guide, use one-fourth the weight of fruit. You may also add about 2 tablespoons fresh lemon juice or Rose Hip Syrup (page 215) per pound of fruit to prevent discoloration.

I find it preferable to preserve small whole fruits or sliced fruits in a sugar syrup, as they tend to keep their shape better than when mixed with dry sugar. Before freezing, simply cover uncooked small whole or

sliced fruits with a simple sugar syrup—light, medium, or heavy, according to taste—or poach the fruit in the syrup. If the fruit is poached, be certain that it is completely cooled before being packed and frozen. Whether the fruit is raw or cooked add 2 tablespoons lemon juice or Rose Hip Syrup to every 2 cups of liquid.

Puréed fruits freeze well. Light-colored ones—for example, apricots and apples—need lemon juice and sugar to help prevent discoloration. Dark berries need only lemon juice, for flavor. It is always best to strain out skins or seeds before freezing purées.

Any vegetables destined for the freezer should first be blanched or thoroughly cooked. The heat stops the activity of the enzymes; as a result, flavor, color, and nutrition are preserved. (Vegetables *can* be frozen without a preliminary blanching but their storage life will be greatly reduced, because, unlike fruits, they are not acidic enough to hold up, raw, under ordinary freezing conditions.) Blanching is the technique of immersing food in boiling water and partially cooking it for up to 2 minutes. Always calculate the blanching time from the moment when the water returns to the boil. Once a vegetable has been blanched, it should be immersed in an ice-water bath,

to arrest the cooking, for the same amount of time. If vegetables are not well chilled before freezing, excess ice crystals will build up in the freezer. Drain and pat dry all vegetables before freezing. If they are packed wet, they will form a solid block in the freezer and will be difficult to use.

It is useful to freeze some vegetables, like green beans and broccoli flowerets, by the dry-pack method. However, most vegetables are just as conveniently stored in plastic bags or containers. It is wise to thoroughly cook leafy vegetables, such as sorrel and spinach, before freezing them, to eliminate all excess moisture. Sauté the leaves in a little butter or blanch and purée them.

The packaging of fruits and vegetables is an equally vital step in assuring the quality of the frozen result. It is absolutely essential to purchase freezer-quality wrapping materials or packaging, which guard against the invasion of moisture and vapors. Stainless steel, rigid plastics, and tempered glass make equally good choices. If ordinary plastic bags, aluminum foil, wax paper, or plastic wrap are used, the food will be exposed to the dry air in the freezer, and this can cause freezer burn.

When filling plastic bags or containers, try to press out as much excess air as possible but leave a "headspace" to allow for expansion during freezing. In general, foods prepared by a dry-pack method require about a half inch, whereas purées, juices, and fruits packed in liquids require about 1 inch. It is also important always to fill a bag or container to capacity; otherwise the food may dry out.

With plastic wraps and aluminum be certain that the wrappings adhere well and that all air bubbles are excluded.

Freeze fruits and vegetables immediately after packaging. Follow the freezer manufacturer's instructions for packing the food into it. Depending on the model, there is

A quiet corner in Rosemary Verey's garden at Barnsley House, Gloucestershire.

always a recommended area where the foods will freeze the fastest—usually near the vent where the cold air enters. Fruits prepared with sugar, and blanched vegetables, will keep in the freezer for up to 12 months. Unsweetened fruits and those with elusive flavors, such as tropical fruits, are best within 3 to 6 months.

When defrosting frozen fruits and vegetables, keep in mind that the food will be better protected under very hot or cold conditions where microorganisms cannot survive. Thaw frozen fruits overnight in the refrigerator, and cook frozen vegetables by plunging them directly into boiling water.

What follows are freezing instructions for specific fruits and vegetables:

FRUITS

Apricots: The best way to treat apricots for freezing is to purée them. To prevent discoloration during the freezing, add ½ cup sugar and 2 tablespoons fresh lemon juice to every 2 cups purée. Once defrosted, the purée can be used as a warm sauce for poached fruit or as a base for soufflés and *bavarois*. When using this sweetened purée in recipes requiring unsweetened apricot purée, sugar adjustments will have to be made.

Blackberries: Freeze blackberries in either an unsweetened purée form or by the dry-pack method if you would like to retain the form of the fruit.

Blueberries: Blueberries are best frozen by the dry-pack method. To use them in cakes, muffins, or pancakes, add the still frozen berries to the batter. They will be more likely to remain whole, and the loss of juice will be reduced. Frozen blueberries are also good as a base for dessert sauces.

Cranberries: Fresh cranberries freeze perfectly well without any extra attention apart from sorting out any bruised or rotten ones. Because cranberries are relatively dry, they can be packed in plastic bags or freezer

Seeding beds in the vast kitchen garden at Little Mythhurst Farm, Horley, Surrey.

containers in their raw state. Always use frozen cranberries in their frozen state. Once defrosted, they become limp and lose their juice.

Currants: red, black, and white: Currants are best frozen by the dry-pack method. Frozen currants are good to have on hand for making jelly. Use the berries directly from the freezer; there is no need to thaw them first.

Elderberries: Elderberries freeze well by the dry-pack method. Remove the berries from the stalk, pick them over, discarding the bruised ones, and rinse and pat them dry before proceeding.

Gooseberries: Gooseberries can be successfully frozen by the dry-pack method and can be used throughout the year for pie fillings or stewed with other fruits to make a winter compote. Use the berries in the frozen state; thawing impairs their texture. Gooseberry juice, which is handy to have on hand for making jams and jellies (see recipe on page 107), freezes beautifully.

Grapes: Grapes can be frozen whole, with or without the skins and are a good snack, straight from the freezer, for children. Freeze the fruit by the dry-pack method. Grape juice concentrate can be frozen and teamed up with low-pectin fruits to make jams and jellies. See Fresh Fig and Vine-Ripened Grape Jam (page 104).

Oranges: The only varieties of orange that are worthwhile preserving in the freezer are Seville and blood oranges. Seville oranges can be frozen whole and used throughout the year for making marmalade. They need no special attention beyond scrubbing and wiping dry. Store the whole oranges in plastic freezer bags for up to one year. Thaw them in the refrigerator overnight before using. The blood orange, which is in the markets for such a short period of time, is worth juicing and freezing to have on hand year round (see page 125).

Peaches and Nectarines: The best way to treat peaches and nectarines for the freezer is to peel, pit, and purée them. To prevent the flesh from discoloring, add ½ cup sugar and 2 tablespoons fresh lemon juice to every 2 cups purée. Avoid freezing white peaches, they are more fragile than the yellow varieties and tend to discolor in spite of the lemon juice treatment. Partially thawed peach and nectarine purées can be swirled into homemade ice cream; use 1 to 2 cups for every quart of ice cream. The purées also make good sauces for bread and rice puddings.

Raspberries: Freeze raspberries as either an unsweetened purée or whole, using the dry-pack method. The whole raspberries will be a little soft when defrosted, but are excellent when added to trifle or *crème brûlée* or used in the classic Russian red fruit kissel pudding.

Strawberries: The best way to freeze strawberries is in purée form. Whole berries do not stand up to the dry-pack method because they contain so much water. They can be sliced and packed with layers of sugar but the result is a somewhat sloppy disappointment.

VEGETABLES

Asparagus: Young tender asparagus spears can be frozen fairly successfully for up to four months. Trim the stalks and blanch the spears in boiling water for 3 minutes. Drain and quickly plunge them into a bowl of ice water to stop the cooking. Pat them dry and store them in plastic freezer bags in convenient portions.

Broccoli flowerets and stems: Broccoli is such a hardy vegetable that it responds well to freezing after blanching. To prepare the vegetable, simply separate the flowerets from the stems and blanch them in a generous quantity of boiling water for 2 minutes. Drain them and immerse them in a bowl of ice water to stop the cooking. Pat dry and set them aside on a tray, leaving space be-

Cardoon plants, in the kitchen garden at Hope End, Herefordshire, are bound in brown paper to keep them white until the harvest.

tween each floweret. Peel the stems and blanch them for 3 minutes. Repeat the draining and refreshing steps and spread them out on another tray. Freeze the broccoli parts for 2 hours, or until frozen solid. Pack in convenient portions in freezer bags.

Cardoons: This stalky vegetable belongs to the thistle family, and the taste is reminiscent of the related globe artichoke. The best way to preserve cardoons is by freezing. The stems must be peeled and blanched before any subsequent cooking or preparation. Cut the stems into 2- to 4-inch pieces and blanch them in boiling water for 3 minutes. Drain them, let them cool, and pat them dry before packing them into freezer containers. If you want to keep the pieces separate, use the dry-pack method. The frozen stalks can be braised directly in a little chicken stock or can be added to soups such as minestrone.

Cauliflower: Cauliflower freezes well and, once packed away as flowerets, it is handy for making delicious gratins, vegetable stews, and soups. Break each head of cauliflower into flowerets, and blanch small quantities in boiling salted water for 2 minutes. Quickly plunge the cauliflower into ice water to stop the cooking. Drain the flowerets and pack them in freezer bags or freeze them by the dry-pack method.

Corn: The best way to freeze the kernels of freshly picked corn is to blanch whole cobs in plenty of boiling salted water for 3 minutes. Drain them and let them cool. Cut the kernels off with a sharp knife and pack them into plastic freezer containers. Since the kernels tend to clump together during freezing, either pack the kernels in convenient portions or use the dry-pack method, freezing the kernels on trays before packing. There is no need to thaw the corn before cooking it.

Green beans: Freezing is an ideal solution for preserving green beans. Trim both ends of each bean and blanch the beans in small batches in a large amount of boiling salted water for 1 minute. Quickly plunge the beans into a bowl of ice water to stop the cooking. Drain the beans and dry them on paper towels. Spread the beans in a single layer on a baking sheet and freeze them for about 1 hour, or until they are very firm. Pack the beans in convenient portions in freezer bags and freeze them for up to nine months. Do not thaw the beans before, or they will lose their crisp texture.

Pumpkin: Pumpkin is best preserved in purée form (see recipe on page 191).

Tomatoes: Fresh tomatoes do not hold up well to freezing; their excessive moisture causes them to collapse. However, any cooked preparation, such as a tomato sauce or purée does freeze well.

Right: The kitchen garden at Barnsley House. Overleaf: The allotment gardens near Ripon in County Durham.

DRYING

Once fresh food is properly dried it is protected from decay because it has been depleted of the moisture necessary for spoilage microorganisms to survive on.

Traditionally the drying of food relied on the sun or wind. Modern technological advances now make it possible to dry food with artificial heat in either an oven or a special food dehydrator. In addition, certain foods can be dried by being hung indoors.

In theory, any food can be dried providing that two criteria are satisfied: a constant temperature of 120° F. to 150° F. (50° C. to 65° C.) and plenty of ventilation.

To illustrate the wide variety of dried food that is commercially available, just consider the range from meat (sausages and Parma ham), fish (salt cod and kippered herring), vegetables (mushrooms, tomatoes) and fruits (raisins, apricots, and prunes) to herbs and dried legumes (chick peas, lentils, and black-eyed peas).

In practice, I recommend that foods to be home-dried be limited to a selection of fruits, vegetables, and aromatics that can be preserved indoors. Although sun and outdoor air-drying produce the truest flavors, the average climate excludes this as a sensible approach. The key to successful drying is to keep the items small, so that they will dry uniformly and quickly. If the drying period is prolonged beyond a day, yeasts, molds, and bacteria can develop.

To dry foods indoors, you can use either the oven method or the air-drying method. For the oven method, very little special equipment is required (although a thermometer can be useful if the temperature of your oven is unreliable). The prepared food will have to be spread out on a wire or wooden rack covered with cheesecloth. Special stacking trays are available commercially, but you can devise your own system

Above: The flowering heads of leeks are dried for decorative use. Right: flowering marjoram.

The fruits that are most successfully dried at home are apples, pears, apricots, and peaches. All have to be peeled, cored or pitted, and sliced into thin wedges or rings to facilitate the drying. To prevent discoloration, the prepared fruit should be dipped in a salt and lemon juice solution before being set out to dry (see Dried Apple Rings, page 65). Small fruits such as cranberries and cherries are also good candidates for drying, and no special treatment, except for the pitting of the cherries, is necessary (see Dried Cherries, page 83, and Dried Cranberries, page 93).

The vegetables that are most successfully dried at home are wild mushrooms (see Dried Forest Mushrooms, page 181) and corn (see Jane's Dried Corn, page 176). Although the corn may require a prolonged period in the oven, the mushrooms are swiftly air-dried indoors.

Aromatic flavorings such as orange peel, herbs, flowers, and chili peppers are also easily dried by being hung in a well-ventilated room.

Once a food has been dried, store it immediately to prevent re-absorption of moisture from the air. Glass storage jars and metal tins are generally the best containers.

Dried fruits and aromatics are most often consumed or added to preparations in their dried state. However, to reconstitute dried fruits and vegetables, soak them in water or another suitable liquid for a few hours before cooking. In the case of fruit compotes, the soaking liquid is delicious when reduced and used as a sauce.

Beds of lavender and rosemary bushes at Benenden Walled Garden, Kent.

51

SPECIAL PACKAGING AND LABELING

The choice of packaging for a preserve is usually dictated by the ingredients and method of preserving. Some preserves contain ingredients that require only simple waxed disks as covers; others require a vacuum seal to exclude air.

All foods to be processed in a water bath need the protection provided by sturdy glass jars with clamp or screw-band lids. These containers are designed (1) to ensure that water cannot permeate the lids during the sterilization process and (2) to allow air to escape during the cooling process. Once the air escapes, a vacuum seal is formed and the sterilized food will remain in good condition for an extended period of time.

WAXED DISKS

Jams and jellies, which have high concentrations of sugar and acid, need only the protection of a waxed disk to prevent spoilage organisms from contaminating them. They are usually covered with a lid or cover to keep dust out. Pre-cut waxed disks and cellophane covers can be purchased in convenient packages. Once a jar is filled with a hot preserve, a waxed disk is placed, waxed-side down, over the entire surface and gently pressed to remove any air bubbles. Cellophane covers can be trimmed to about ¾ inch larger than the diameter of the rim, dampened on top to help stretch the surface, and fastened to the jar with a rubber band. Alternatively, an attractive circle of cloth can be applied and secured with ribbon. Apply this second seal only when the preserve is very hot or completely cold. Moisture will condense and could encourage the growth of molds if a temperature between the extremes is sealed off.

A collection of French sealing wax, seals, decorative stamps and ribbons for packaging preserves.

PARAFFIN

Chutneys contain such a significant amount of vinegar that the main concern with covering them is to prevent evaporation and shrinkage rather than spoilage. The most effective way to achieve this is with a seal of paraffin wax. Paraffin can be purchased in either block or candle form. It is best to melt the wax in an old, clean tin can set in a water bath. Before pouring, secure the can with tongs.

Jars to be covered with paraffin should be filled to within ¼ inch of the rim. Place a waxed disk directly on the hot surface and smooth out any air bubbles. Pour in a layer of paraffin, just enough to reach the level of the rim. Let the paraffin cool completely before storing. If you like, protect the paraffin from dust with either a cellophane or a cloth cover. The paraffin can also be applied when the preserve is completely cool. As with jams and jellies, do not cover warm foods as the temperature provides breeding ground for molds.

To break the paraffin seal, simply insert the tip of a sharp knife between the paraffin and the jar and gently pry it off. Generally the paraffin can be re-placed on the preserve until the contents are depleted.

CORKS AND SEALING WAX

Corks provide a neat sealing solution for preserves in long-necked bottles. The cork is sturdy enough to withstand sterilization in a water bath for those preserves that require heat treatment and are equally serviceable for sealing simple preserves such as Crème de Cassis (page 99) and vinegars, which do not need to be sterilized.

Before use, all corks need to be soaked in warm water for at least 15 minutes to eliminate any dust and to render them more supple. To insert the cork into a bottle, use either a special corker or apply a few gentle taps with the broad side of a wooden mallet. If the contents of the bottle are to be sterilized, allow the cork to remain ¼ inch above the rim of the jar. For all other preserves, level the cork with the rim.

For sterilization, the cork will have to be secured with a string; otherwise the pressure that builds up in the bottles will expel the cork. Simply make a crossed indentation on the top of the cork with a sharp knife, then tie the cork down with a piece of string, using the indents in the cork as anchors. Once the jar is sterilized and cooled, remove the string and force the cork down to the level of the rim.

To complete the seal on the corks, for both sterilized and non-sterilized bottles, dip the neck into melted sealing wax. The wax provides an airtight enclosure and makes an attractive finish to any homemade preserve. Sealing wax can be purchased in a variety of colors and generally in stick form at stationery/art supply stores. As with paraffin, carefully melt the sealing wax in an old clean tin can set in a water bath.

To break a seal, chip away at the sealing wax with the dull side of a small knife and pull the cork out with a corkscrew. Alternatively, carefully rotate the neck of the bottle over a low flame, just long enough to soften the wax. Scrape the wax off with an old knife and proceed with the corkscrew.

LABELS

It is essential to label all preserves with the contents and date of fabrication. As obvious as this information may be at the moment of preparation, the facts fade in the memory over a period of a few months. It is wise to keep most preserves no longer than one year, and the label will serve you well in the tracking of time.

To make your preserves more attractive, collect interesting labels and tags, pieces of fabric, ribbons, and string and keep them on hand for these projects.

Brightly colored labels and cotton fabrics can be used to add a personal note to homemade preserves.

CLASSIC APPLE CHARLOTTE

Serve this traditional French dessert with lightly sweetened whipped cream or a custard sauce.

    4 cups Simply Good Applesauce
        (page 62)
    1½ sticks (¾ cup) unsalted butter
    ¾ cup firmly packed light brown sugar
    1 teaspoon ground cinnamon
    2 tablespoons Calvados, if desired
    12 slices white bread, slightly stale or
        dried in the oven and the crusts
        removed

In a large saucepan cook the applesauce with ½ stick of the butter, the brown sugar, cinnamon, and Calvados over low heat, stirring, until the sugar is dissolved. Taste for seasoning.

Line the bottom of a 1-quart charlotte mold with a buttered round of wax paper. Cut 8 slices of the bread into 1½-inch-wide fingers. Cut the remaining 4 slices into semicircles that will cover the bottom and top of the mold.

Melt the remaining 1 stick of butter over low heat in a wide shallow pan, dip 2 of the semicircles of bread in the butter, and arrange them on the bottom of the mold. Dip the bread fingers in the butter and overlap them along the sides of the mold. Fill the mold with the applesauce mixture and cover the top with the remaining semicircles, dipped in the butter.

Bake the charlotte in a preheated 400° oven for 15 minutes. Reduce the heat to 350° and continue baking for 30 minutes, or until the bread is golden and firm.

Let the charlotte cool in the mold on a rack for 15 minutes. Unmold the dessert and serve it hot or at room temperature.

Serves 4 to 6

GRACE STUCK'S
APPLESAUCE FRUITCAKE

I have never had the pleasure of meeting Grace Stuck from Minnesota, but her granddaughter, Susan Stuck, is a good friend of mine and has shared this recipe with me and other friends. This cake has now become a Christmas classic among us.

 3 cups Simply Good Applesauce
     (page 62)
 2 sticks (1 cup) unsalted butter
 1 cup firmly packed brown sugar
 ¼ cup unsulphured molasses
 ¼ cup honey
 4 cups all-purpose flour
 1 teaspoon baking powder
 1 teaspoon ground cinnamon
 1 teaspoon ground cardamom
 1 teaspoon freshly grated nutmeg
 1 teaspoon ground ginger
 1 teaspoon salt
 1 pound raisins
 1 pound dried pears, coarsely chopped
 1½ cups dried apricots, coarsely
     chopped
 1½ cups pitted dates, coarsely
     chopped
 1½ cups chopped toasted walnuts,
     plus 1 cup walnut halves
 1½ cups chopped toasted and skinned
     hazelnuts
 1 cup brandy

In a large saucepan heat the applesauce over moderate heat. Add the butter, a few tablespoons at a time, stirring, until it is incorporated. Bring the applesauce just to a boil, stirring constantly.

Remove the pan from the heat and stir in the brown sugar, molasses, and honey, stirring until the sugar is dissolved. Transfer the mixture to a large bowl and let it cool.

Sift together the flour, baking powder, cinnamon, cardamom, nutmeg, ginger, and salt. Stir the flour mixture into the applesauce. Fold in the dried fruit, the chopped nuts, and ½ cup of the brandy.

Divide the batter among 4 buttered and floured 9 x 5-inch loaf pans and decorate the top of each loaf with the walnut halves.

Bake the cakes in a preheated 275° oven for 1½ hours, or until a skewer inserted in the center of each loaf comes out clean and hot to the touch. Let the cakes cool in the pans on racks and then invert them onto the racks to cool completely.

Wrap the cakes in cheesecloth and brush them liberally with the remaining ½ cup brandy until the cheesecloth is soaked. Wrap the cakes in foil and store them in a cool dry place. The cakes keep for 3 to 4 months. For added flavor brush the cakes with additional brandy every month.

Makes four 9 x 5-inch loaves

Homemade applesauce is an essential ingredient for Grace Stuck's Applesauce Fruitcake. The fruitcakes receive a brushing of brandy before wrapping and storing.

SIMPLY GOOD APPLESAUCE

This applesauce is preserved without any sugar or spices. It can be sweetened and flavored according to subsequent use.

6 cups unsweetened apple juice or
   cider
5 pounds cooking apples, quartered
Pinch of salt

In a large preserving pan bring the apple juice or cider to a boil over high heat and reduce it by half.

Add the apple quarters to the pan with the salt, bring the liquid back to a boil, and simmer the fruit, stirring to prevent sticking, for 45 minutes, or until it is reduced to a purée.

Pass the purée through a fine sieve set over a bowl to remove the peel, core, and seeds. Ladle the applesauce into three warm 1-quart jars and seal. Process the jars in a boiling water bath for 10 minutes. Let the jars cool completely before checking the seals and storing.

Makes 3 quarts

GLAZED PORK LOIN WITH PRESERVED LADY APPLES

Dried apple rings may be substituted for the Lady Apples Steeped in Spiced Cider, in which case apple cider or apple juice is substituted for the spiced cider.

2 garlic cloves
1 teaspoon crumbled dried sage
1 teaspoon crumbled dried rosemary
5-pound boneless pork loin, untied
2 tablespoons all-purpose flour
Salt
2 tablespoons vegetable oil
1 onion, quartered
2 carrots
1 quart Lady Apples Steeped in Spiced
   Cider (at right), drained, reserving
   2 cups of the juice
1 Bouquet Garni (page 237)
½ cup heavy cream
1 tablespoon dry mustard
Freshly ground pepper

In a mortar with a pestle crush the garlic with the sage and rosemary to obtain a smooth paste. Make small slits with a sharp knife all over the pork loin and insert the paste into them. Tie the pork into a uniform roll with kitchen string and set aside for several hours at room temperature or overnight in the refrigerator.

Sprinkle the pork with the flour and salt to taste. In a deep flameproof casserole heat the oil until it is hot but not smoking and brown the pork on all sides in the oil. Transfer the pork to a plate and discard all but 1 tablespoon of the fat from the casserole. Add the onion quarters and whole carrots to the casserole and cook them over moderate heat until they are slightly browned.

Add the 2 cups spiced cider and bring it to a boil, scraping up any browned bits. Add the pork and the bouquet garni, bring the liquid slowly back to a boil, and simmer the mixture, covered, for about 15 minutes.

Braise the mixture in a preheated 350° oven, basting frequently, for 1 hour. Add the preserved lady apples to the mixture and continue cooking the mixture, uncovered, basting frequently, for 30 minutes.

Transfer the pork to a cutting board and let it rest, covered with foil, for 20 minutes. Transfer the apples to a plate with a slotted spoon and keep them warm. Discard the bouquet garni, onion, and carrot.

Boil the cooking liquid, reducing it by half. In a small bowl combine the cream and mustard and whisk the mixture into the reduced liquid. Taste for seasonings, adding salt and freshly ground pepper if desired, and strain the sauce through a sieve into a heated sauceboat.

Discard the strings from the pork and carve the roast into ¼-inch slices. Arrange the pork on a platter with the apples and pass the sauce separately.

Serves 6

LADY APPLES STEEPED IN SPICED CIDER

Pickled apples can be served cold with ham or leftover cold pork roast; they are equally delicious when served as a warm garnish for roasts. The spiced cider can be used as a braising liquid and reduced to form the base of a sauce.

4 cups apple cider
2 cups cider vinegar
½-inch-thick slice of fresh ginger
1 tablespoon allspice berries
2½ cups sugar
4 pounds lady apples (whole with stems)
3 whole cinnamon sticks

In a large nonreactive saucepan, combine the cider, vinegar, ginger, allspice, and sugar. Heat the mixture over low heat, stirring until the sugar is dissolved. Increase the heat and boil the syrup for 10 minutes.

Add the apples to the syrup and simmer them for 10 minutes. Transfer the apples to three warm 1-quart jars with a slotted spoon and insert a cinnamon stick into each jar. Boil the cider mixture for 10 minutes more, strain it, and divide it among the jars.

Process the jars in a boiling water bath for 15 minutes. Let the jars cool completely before checking the seals and storing.

Makes 3 quarts

APPLE PECTIN STOCK

The skin, flesh, and seeds of cooking apples and crabapples contain a large amount of pectin, which can be extracted and used to help set jams and jellies made with fruits that are low in this natural substance. It is a good idea to make large quantities of the stock in the autumn, when apples are at their peak. Since ½ cup of pectin stock will set 4 cups of fruit or fruit juice, store your pectin in amounts that will be useful for your general needs. The pectin can be frozen or sterilized and kept for up to 1 year.

12 pounds cooking apples or crabapples or a mixture of both

Scrub the apples, discarding any leaves or stems, and coarsely chop them, including skin, core, and seeds.

In a large preserving pan combine the apples with 3 quarts water (the apples should be barely covered). Bring the water to a boil over moderate heat and simmer the apples for 20 to 30 minutes, or until they are softened.

Tip the contents of the pan into a dampened jelly bag set over a large bowl and let it drain for 24 hours.

Transfer the strained liquid back to the preserving pan and boil it over high heat until it is reduced by half or a large clot forms when the pectin level is tested (see Testing the Pectin Level on page 26).

Ladle the stock into ½- to 1-cup jars or freezer containers. (For a really clear stock, pour the reduced pectin stock through a sieve lined with dampened cheesecloth before ladling it into containers.) If you are not freezing the stock, seal the jars and process them in a water bath for 5 minutes.

Makes 2½ quarts

DRIED APPLE RINGS

The drying method indicated below for the apple rings can also be applied to pears, peaches, and apricots. The dried fruit can be eaten as it is, or soaked and stewed in water, fruit juice, or wine if you want to make a compote.

2 teaspoons salt
½ cup fresh lemon juice
7 to 8 pounds cooking apples

In a large bowl combine the salt and lemon juice with 1½ quarts water.

Peel and core the apples, leaving them whole (it may be best to proceed in small batches to prevent discoloration). Slice the apples into ¼-inch rings, put them in the acidulated water, and let them soak for at least 10 minutes.

Transfer the slices in batches with a slotted spoon to paper towels to drain, pat them dry, and arrange them in a single layer on wire racks covered with a double thickness of cheesecloth.

Put the racks of apples in a cold oven, set the oven to 120°, and when it reaches that temperature, wedge a fork or spoon in the oven door to keep it ajar. Then raise the temperature to 150° and dry the apples for 4 to 5 hours, or until the apples exude no water when they are squeezed. (The fruit should still be soft and pliable.) Let the fruit cool completely for several hours or overnight. Pack the apples in jars or metal tins lined with wax paper.

Makes 2 pounds

Early morning sun passing over an espallied apple tree at Northcut on the Isle of Wight. This fruit tree is reputed to be over 100 years old.

PURE APPLE BUTTER WITH CARDAMOM

Use a tart variety of apple for this butter; the brown sugar and cider will temper the acidity. If available, use a mixture of windfalls, including some crabapples.

6 to 8 pounds tart apples
3 cups unsweetened apple cider
2 cups firmly packed light brown sugar
1 tablespoon ground cardamom
2 teaspoons ground cinnamon
1 teaspoon freshly grated lemon zest
Pinch of salt

Coarsely chop the apples, including the peel, seeds, and cores. Combine the apples with the cider in a large preserving pan and bring the mixture to a boil over low heat, stirring constantly. Cook the mixture over moderate heat for about 30 minutes, or until the apples are softened.

Pass the apples through a sieve set over a bowl, pressing on the solids with a spoon. Discard peel, seeds, and cores, and return the purée to a cleaned preserving pan.

Add the brown sugar, cardamom, cinnamon, zest, and salt to the purée and simmer the mixture for 30 to 45 minutes, or until it is thickened.

Ladle the "butter" into warm jars and seal. Process the jars in a boiling water bath for 10 minutes. Let the jars cool completely before checking the seals and storing.

Makes 4 to 5 cups

APPLE BUTTER AND APPLE TART

Basic Shortcrust Dough for one 12-inch tart (page 234)
2 cups Pure Apple Butter with Cardamom (at left)
3 to 4 cooking apples, peeled, cored, and thinly sliced
½ cup Apricot Jam (page 68)

Fit the dough into a 12-inch tart pan with a removable rim, prick the shell all over and chill for 30 minutes. Line the shell with foil, fill with pie weights or dried beans, and bake in a preheated 350° oven for 10 to 12 minutes, or until it is set and light golden. Remove the pie weights and let the shell cool slightly.

Spread the apple butter over the bottom of the shell and on it arrange the apple slices in an attractive pattern. Bake the tart in the 350° oven for 20 to 25 minutes, or until the apples are soft and the pastry golden. Let the tart cool on a wire rack.

Strain the jam through a sieve into a small saucepan and heat it over low heat until it is of spreading consistency. Brush the apple slices with glaze.

Serves 8

Preserved fruit is ideally suited for making baked goods. Here, clockwise from the top: Cherry Clafouti made with Pitted Cherries in Almond Syrup, Apple Tart made with a base of Pure Apple Butter with Cardamom, Black Cherry Jam Tart with Lattice Crust made with Black Cherry Jam and fresh apples, and Glazed Apricot Tart made with Whole Apricots in Vanilla Syrup.

GLAZED APRICOT TART

Sweet Rich Pastry Dough for one 8- to
   10-inch tart (page 234)
3 cups drained Whole Apricots in
   Vanilla Syrup (page 69)
⅓ cup sugar

Fit the dough into a 9-inch tart pan with a
removable rim, prick the shell all over and
chill for 20 to 30 minutes. Line the shell
with foil, fill with pie weights or dried
beans, and bake in a preheated 375° oven
for 15 minutes, or until it is set and light
golden. Remove the pie weights. Leave the
oven on.

Quarter the apricots, discarding the pits.
Arrange the apricot quarters, cut-sides up,
in a circle in the shell, sprinkle them with
the sugar, and bake the tart in the 375° oven
for 15 minutes, or until the apricots are
glazed and browned lightly.

Let the tart cool on a wire rack and serve
it warm or at room temperature.

Serves 6 to 8

HUNZA APRICOT HONEY

Dried Hunza apricots can be purchased in
specialty shops or health food stores. The
fruit is from the Hunza Valley in Kashmir.
Unlike most dried apricots, Hunzas are
whole and unpitted and are about the size
of a small plum. The fruit is very sweet,
and the flavor is best described as a combination of apricots and peaches.

2 pounds dried Hunza apricots
2 tablespoons fresh lemon juice
½ cup honey

In a large bowl cover the apricots with 4
cups boiling-hot water and soak for several
hours. Drain the apricots, reserving the liquid, pit them, and coarsely chop them.

In a preserving pan boil the reserved liquid over high heat until it is reduced to 2
cups. Add the apricots and lemon juice and
boil the fruit for 20 to 30 minutes, or until it
is softened.

Pass the mixture through a sieve set over
a bowl, pressing hard with a wooden spoon.
Transfer the purée back to the pan, and
cook the mixture with the honey for 10
minutes, or until it remains separated when
the spoon is scraped across the bottom of
the pan. Taste for sweetness.

Ladle the apricot honey into warm jars
and seal. Process the jars in a boiling water
bath: 5 minutes for jars up to 1 pint, 10
minutes for jars up to 1 quart. Let the jars
cool completely before checking the seals
and storing.

Makes 1 quart

APRICOT JAM

This is a simple, straightforward method for
making apricot preserves. Slightly under-
ripe apricots will give a jam with better taste
and texture.

6 pounds firm-ripe apricots
About 2½ pounds (about 5 cups) sugar
2 tablespoons fresh lemon juice

Quarter the apricots with a small knife and
pit them. Crack open three of the pits and
reserve the kernels. Weigh the apricots and
measure ½ pound (about 1 cup) sugar for
every 1 pound fruit.

In a preserving pan combine the measured sugar with 1 cup water and the lemon
juice and cook the mixture over low heat,
stirring, until the sugar is melted. Bring the
syrup to a boil and add the apricots. Bring
the syrup back to a boil and cook the apricots for about 20 minutes, or until they are
very soft but not mushy.

With a slotted spoon divide the apricots

among three warm sterilized 1-quart jars, filling each jar three-quarters full, and reserving the syrup.

Boil the syrup over high heat for about 15 minutes, or until the jellying point is reached.

Split the reserved apricot kernels in half and add 2 to each jar. Pour the boiling-hot syrup over the apricots and seal the jars.

Makes 3 quarts

WHOLE APRICOTS IN VANILLA SYRUP

These apricots can be served unadorned or in custard-based tarts. Or use them in place of the peaches in Whole Preserved Peaches with Pistachio Cream (page 131).

4 to 5 pounds firm-ripe apricots
5 cups sugar
½ cup fresh lemon juice
2 vanilla beans, split lengthwise

Plunge the apricots into a large pan of boiling water, bring the liquid back to a boil, and transfer the apricots to a large bowl of cold water. Drain the fruit and let it cool. Peel the apricots if possible; however, there is no need to struggle, because the skin often comes off later in the cooking process.

While the apricots are cooling, in a saucepan combine the sugar, lemon juice, and 2½ cups water and heat the mixture over a low heat, stirring frequently, until the sugar is dissolved. Bring the syrup to a boil and add the apricots. Return the syrup to a boil and simmer the apricots for 10 minutes. Discard the skins if they have slipped from the fruit during cooking.

With a slotted spoon divide the apricots between two warm 1½-quart jars, reserving the syrup. Add 2 vanilla bean halves to each jar.

Boil the syrup over high heat for about 5

minutes in order to reduce any additional liquid exuded from the apricots. Pour the syrup over the apricots, seal the jars, and process in a boiling water bath for 20 minutes. Let the jars cool completely before checking the seals and storing.

Makes 3 quarts

Whole Apricots in Vanilla Syrup make a simple dessert on their own or served with small cakes or cookies.

TRUE BLUEBERRY JAM

This is the simplest method for making a true berry-flavored jam, provided that the berries are picked fresh and very flavorful. Be warned, though, the jam can be a little runny.

> 3 pounds blueberries, rinsed
> 4 cups sugar
> 1 teaspoon freshly grated lemon zest
> 2 tablespoons fresh lemon juice

In a preserving pan cook the berries over high heat, stirring constantly with a wooden spoon and crushing them with the back of the spoon, for 5 minutes. (The water left clinging to the berries from washing them will be enough to prevent them from scorching.)

Add the sugar, zest, and juice and cook the mixture over a low heat, stirring, until the sugar is dissolved. Increase the heat to moderate and boil the jam, skimming frequently, for 15 minutes, or until the jellying point is reached.

Remove the preserving pan from the heat and let the jam stand for 10 minutes. Ladle the jam into warm sterilized jars and seal.

Makes 1½ quarts

Freshly picked blueberries from Trehane Orchards in Dorset. The cultivation of blueberries is not widely practiced in England; however, the acid soil in this region is ideally suited to growing these plants. The bushes will grow to a height of six feet and will live for fifty years or more with attentive care and good pruning.

CHERRY CLAFOUTI

The classic French cherry *clafouti* is made from fresh unpitted cherries. The recipe originated in the Limousin region of France, where batter and fruit desserts are common. The pitted preserved cherries used here are a good alternative to the fresh, as are any other small fruits such as apricots, prunes, raisins, or plums.

> 2 large whole eggs plus 1 large egg yolk
> 2 cups milk
> ¼ cup unsalted butter, melted and cooled
> ¼ cup plus 2 tablespoons granulated sugar
> ¾ cup all-purpose flour
> Pinch of salt
> 2 cups drained Pitted Cherries in Almond Syrup (page 87)
> Confectioners' sugar, for dusting

In a large bowl combine the whole eggs, yolk, milk, and butter and beat them until the mixture is well combined. Stir in ¼ cup of the granulated sugar, the flour, and salt, stirring until the mixture is just combined.

Spread the cherries in a generously buttered 9-inch baking dish (6-cup capacity), sprinkled with the remaining 2 tablespoons granulated sugar, and pour the batter over the fruit.

Bake the *clafouti* in a preheated 375° oven for 30 minutes, or until it is puffy, browned on top, and a skewer inserted in the center comes out clean and hot to the touch. Let the *clafouti* cool for 15 to 20 minutes before serving. (The batter will rise like a soufflé and collapse to its original volume as it cools.) Sprinkle the *clafouti* with confectioners' sugar.

Serves 6 to 8

BLACK CHERRY JAM TART WITH LATTICE CRUST

The cherry jam in this tart is combined with cooking apples to cut the sweetness and add texture to the filling.

Basic Shortcrust Dough for one 12-inch tart (page 234)
2 tablespoons unsalted butter
2 cooking apples, peeled, cored, and coarsely chopped
2 tablespoons fresh lemon juice
1½ cups Black Cherry Jam (at right)
Egg wash made by beating 1 large egg yolk with 2 tablespoons water
Confectioners' sugar, for dusting

Roll out three-fourths of the dough and fit it into a 12 × 8-inch baking dish, leaving a decorative edge. Prick the shell all over and chill it for 20 minutes.

While the shell is being chilled, heat the butter in a sauté pan over moderate heat until it sizzles, add the apples and lemon juice, and sauté the apples until they are golden and all the moisture is evaporated. Remove the pan from the heat, stir in the black cherry jam, and let the filling cool.

Roll out the remaining dough ⅛ inch thick and cut it into ½-inch-wide strips.

Spoon the filling into the shell, brush the edge of the shell with some of the egg wash, and lay the strips of dough across the filling in a simple lattice pattern. Trim any excess dough and pinch the edges together. Brush the strips with the remaining egg wash. Bake the tart in a preheated 350° oven for 45 minutes, or until the lattice is golden brown. Let the tart cool slightly and sprinkle it with confectioners' sugar.

Serves 6 to 8

BLACK CHERRY JAM

Cherries are very low in pectin, which means that most attempts to make jam from them will not be successful unless a pectin-rich substance is added. Apple Pectin Stock is the best natural and neutrally flavored source, although red currant jelly (Red Currant Magic on page 96) can be used for a more complex flavor.

4 cups sugar
1¾ cups Apple Pectin Stock (page 63)
4 pounds dark sweet cherries, such as Bing
2 tablespoons kirsch, if desired

In a preserving pan dissolve the sugar in the apple pectin stock over low heat, stirring occasionally to keep the sugar from sticking.

Pit the cherries with either a cherry/olive pitter (available in kitchen supply shops) or by halving the cherries and squeezing out the pits. Tie several of the pits in a piece of cheesecloth and crack them with a rolling pin. Add the cheesecloth bag to the preserving pan.

Bring the syrup in the preserving pan to a boil and add the pitted cherries. Bring the syrup back to a boil, cook the mixture rapidly, skimming the jam frequently, for 15 minutes, or until the jellying point is reached. Let it cool for 15 minutes. Discard the bag of cracked pits.

Stir in the kirsch. Ladle the jam into warm sterilized jars and seal.

Makes 1½ quarts

Black Cherry Jam bubbling away on a traditional English Aga stove.

DRIED CHERRIES

Dried cherries have been widely available commercially only for the past couple of years. However, the concept is certainly not a new one. In Menon's *La Cuisinière Bourgeoise*, first published in 1746, the author includes a method for drying whole cherries with pit and stem intact. While his method may produce a more decorative effect, I prefer to pit and stem the cherries so that they are ready for subsequent preparations. Dried cherries can be used like raisins: They can be eaten alone as a snack or added to cookie and cake batters as is or after being plumped in a liquid.

  5 pounds dark sweet cherries, such as
    Bing

Cover enough wire cooling racks with a layer of dampened cheesecloth to accommodate all the cherries in a single layer. Pit the cherries, either with a cherry/olive pitter (available in kitchen supply shops) or by halving them. Place the cherries or cherry halves, cut-sides up, on the cloth-covered racks.

Put the racks of cherries in a cold oven, set the oven to 120°, and when it reaches that temperature, wedge a fork or spoon in the oven door to keep it ajar. Then raise the temperature to 150° and dry the cherries for 2 hours.

Turn the cherries over and continue drying them for at least another 2 hours, or until they are shriveled and dry to the touch when squeezed.

Remove the cherries from the oven and let them cool. Store in jars or an airtight tin.

Makes 2 to 2½ pounds

A prized morello cherry tree against the kitchen garden wall at Rodmarton Manor, Gloucestershire.

DRIED CHERRY AND TOASTED ALMOND BISCOTTI

My Aunt Evelyn finally parted with her recipe for Italian filled cookies. It was given to her by her Italian mother-in-law over thirty years ago. Although my aunt may not approve of the "gourmet" substitute of dried cherries for candied ones, I think they make a wonderful—and healthy—change. Because these *biscotti* are not very sweet they are nice to have on hand to serve with a glass of sweet wine for impromptu afternoon visitors.

½ cup Dried Cherries (page 83)
2 tablespoons kirsch
1 stick (½ cup) unsalted butter,
    softened
1 cup sugar
4 large eggs
Pinch of pod vanilla grains
3 cups all-purpose flour
1 heaping teaspoon baking powder
Pinch of salt
1 cup whole blanched almonds,
    toasted, cooled and coarsely chopped
Egg wash, made from 1 large egg
    beaten lightly with a pinch of salt

In a small bowl plump the cherries in the kirsch for 1 hour.

In a bowl with an electric mixer cream the butter with ½ cup of the sugar until the mixture is light and fluffy. Beat in the eggs, one at a time, making sure that each one is fully incorporated before adding the next. Beat in the vanilla grains.

Sift together the flour, baking powder, and salt. Fold the dry ingredients into the creamed mixture, stir in the nuts, and form the mixture into a round. Cover the dough with plastic wrap and chill it for 30 minutes.

Divide the dough into quarters. Sprinkle 2 tablespoons of the remaining sugar on a work surface and form one quarter into a 12-inch-long log (about 1½ inches in diameter). Make an indentation with the side of your hand down the center of the log and fill it with 2 tablespoons of the cherries (the cherries should have absorbed all the kirsch; if not, pat them dry). Pinch the dough together and roll the log a few times to completely seal the seam. Transfer the log to a buttered baking sheet.

Repeat the process of rolling and filling with the remaining dough, sugar, and cherries. Transfer the logs to the baking sheet.

Brush the tops of the logs with the egg wash and bake the logs in a preheated 375° oven for 20 minutes, or until they are lightly golden. Let the logs cool on the sheet on a rack for 10 minutes. Leave the oven on.

Transfer the logs to a cutting board and cut them into ½-inch-thick diagonal slices. Return the *biscotti* to the baking sheet, cut-sides down, and bake them for 20 minutes, or until they are golden brown. Let the *biscotti* cool on racks and store them in airtight containers. The *biscotti* keep for up to 3 weeks.

Makes 60 *biscotti*

To make Dried Cherry and Toasted Almond Biscotti, long rolls of cherry-filled biscotti dough are baked until golden, then sliced and baked a second time. The Italian word for these traditional cookies literally means twice-baked.

PITTED CHERRIES IN ALMOND SYRUP

These cherries are a blessing to have on hand for pie or strudel fillings, or even as an ice cream topping.

  4 pounds dark sour cherries
  4 cups sugar

Pit the cherries as neatly as possible (a special device for pitting cherries and olives is available in most kitchen supply shops). Tie several of the pits in a piece of cheesecloth and crack them with a rolling pin.

In a large saucepan combine the sugar with 2 quarts water and cook the mixture over low heat, stirring, until the sugar is dissolved. Add the bag of cracked pits, which will impart an almond flavor, bring the syrup to a boil, and boil it for 5 minutes.

Add the cherries, cook the mixture over moderate heat for about 5 minutes, and transfer the cherries to warm jars with a slotted spoon.

Boil the syrup for 5 minutes, or until it is reduced slightly. Remove the cheesecloth bag, pour the syrup over the cherries, and seal the jars. Process the jars in a boiling water bath: 15 minutes for jars up to 1 pint, 20 minutes for jars up to 1 quart. Let the jars cool completely before checking the seals and storing.

Makes 4 quarts

Freshly picked black cherries have been pitted in preparation for making Black Cherry Jam.

WHITE CHOCOLATE MOUSSE WITH BLACK CHERRY JAM AND CHOCOLATE LEAVES

This mousse is also good with either a Raspberry Purée (page 151) or whole preserved fruit, such as Blood Oranges in Fresh Mint Syrup (page 129) or Pitted Cherries in Almond Syrup (at left).

  12 ounces white chocolate
  3 cups heavy cream
  5 large egg yolks
  ½ cup sugar
  1 tablespoon unflavored gelatin
  3 to 4 tablespoons kirsch
  About ½ cup Black Cherry Jam
    (page 80)
  16 to 20 Chocolate Leaves (page 88)

Chop the white chocolate into small pieces, melt it in a double boiler over simmering water, stirring gently, and let it cool.

Whip all but 2 tablespoons of the cream until soft peaks form and set aside in a cool place. In a large bowl beat the egg yolks until they are thick and pale, beat in the sugar gradually, and continue beating until the mixture is thickened.

In a small bowl let the gelatin soften in 2 tablespoons water and stir in the remaining 2 tablespoons cream. Add the gelatin mixture and the kirsch to the egg mixture.

Carefully fold in the cooled melted chocolate and the whipped cream. Chill the mousse for at least 8 hours or overnight.

To serve, dip 2 serving spoons into a saucepan of boiling-hot water and use them to shape a large scoop of the mousse into an egg form. Repeat the shaping procedure, transferring the mousse to dessert plates as the "eggs" are formed, and garnish each plate with a generous spoonful of the jam and a few chocolate leaves.

Serves 8 to 10

Egg-shaped scoops of white chocolate mousse are served with Black Cherry Jam and Chocolate Leaves for a special dessert. The mousse is equally good with a red fruit purée, such as raspberry or strawberry.

CHOCOLATE LEAVES

Couverture (or covering) chocolate is called for here because it does not melt as easily at room temperature as other chocolates and will hold the leaf shape better.

4 ounces bittersweet chocolate, preferably couverture chocolate
24 firm, nonpoisonous green leaves with stems attached

In a double boiler melt the chocolate over simmering water, stirring. Remove it from the heat.

Drag one side of each leaf across the surface of the chocolate, being careful not to let the chocolate spread to the other side or onto the stem. Arrange the chocolate-coated leaves, chocolate-sides up, on wire racks that have been covered with wax paper. Chill the leaves for at least 30 minutes, or until the chocolate is firm.

To peel off the chocolate, hold the green leaves by the stems and gently pull them away. If the chocolate begins to soften, chill the coated leaves to firm them up.

Makes 24 chocolate leaves

SPIRITED MORELLO CHERRIES

Morello cherries are most noted for their dark red juice and sour taste. They are often referred to as pie cherries because they hold up well to cooking and are enhanced by the addition of sugar. Serve these spirited cherries with some of the kirsch in individual compote dishes. Or use them as a filling in tarts and strudels.

4 pounds morello cherries with ½ inch of each stem intact
About 3 cups sugar
2 cinnamon sticks, each broken into 3 pieces

A few blades of mace
8 cups kirsch

Divide the cherries among six 1-pint jars, alternating layers of the cherries with the sugar (approximately ½ cup sugar per ¾ pound cherries).

Tuck a piece of both mace and cinnamon in the center of each jar, cover the cherry mixture with the kirsch, and seal the jars. Store the unopened jars in a cool, dark place for at least 2 months before eating.

Makes 3 quarts

SPIRITED MORELLO CHERRIES DIPPED IN CHOCOLATE

Chocolate-covered cherries are always welcome when served at the end of a meal with strong black coffee.

5 ounces bittersweet chocolate,
   coarsely chopped
¼ cup heavy cream
1 to 2 tablespoons unsalted butter
24 Spirited Morello Cherries (above),
   drained

In a small saucepan melt the chocolate in the cream over low heat. Remove the pan from the heat and beat in 1 tablespoon of the butter.

Line a wire rack with wax paper. Hold each cherry by the stem, dip it into the chocolate, coating it completely, and set it on the rack. If the chocolate gets too thick, heat it slightly and beat in the remaining 1 tablespoon butter.

Chill the cherries for about 2 hours, or until the chocolate is set. The cherries keep, covered and refrigerated, for 2 days.

Makes 24

CHESTNUT BREAD PUDDING

This is a rich winter dessert that is best served warm with a hot custard or chocolate sauce.

8 slices of homemade-style white
   bread or brioche, crusts discarded
½ stick (¼ cup) unsalted butter,
   softened
½ cup raisins
½ cup finely chopped semisweet
   chocolate
3 large eggs
2 cups Chestnut Jam (page 90)
1 cup milk
1 cup heavy cream
½ teaspoon ground cinnamon
2 tablespoons brandy

Spread one side of the bread slices with the butter and cut each slice into 2 triangles. Arrange 8 triangles, buttered-sides down, in one layer in an 8-inch square baking dish. Sprinkle the bread with the raisins and chocolate and cover with the remaining triangles, buttered-sides down.

In a bowl whisk the eggs, 1 at a time, into the chestnut jam and blend in the milk, cream, cinnamon, and brandy. Pour the mixture over the bread and chill, covered, for at least 8 hours or overnight.

Put the baking dish in a larger dish and add enough boiling water to the larger one to reach halfway up the sides of the baking dish. Bake the pudding in the middle of a preheated 350° oven for 45 minutes, or until a skewer inserted in the center comes out clean. Let the pudding cool in the dish on a wire rack for at least 20 minutes.

Serves 6

CRANBERRY, PEAR, AND PECAN CONSERVE

This conserve livens up cold leftover poultry or can be used in tarts or over ice cream.

1 pound cranberries
4 pounds firm-ripe pears, peeled, cored, and coarsely chopped
2 oranges, unpeeled, seeded, and coarsely chopped
5 cups firmly packed light brown sugar
1 teaspoon ground cinnamon
¼ teaspoon ground cardamom
2 cups Muscat raisins

½ pound pecans, coarsely chopped

In a large bowl combine all the ingredients except the pecans. Let the mixture stand, covered, overnight.

Transfer the fruit to a preserving pan and bring to a boil over low heat. Simmer the fruit, stirring frequently, for 30 minutes. Bring the mixture back to a boil and boil it for 15 minutes, or until it is very thick. Let cool for 15 minutes.

Stir in the pecans. Ladle the conserve into warm sterilized jars and seal.

Makes 2 quarts

94

CRANBERRY NECTAR

Nectars can be enjoyed straight or diluted with sparkling water.

    6 pounds cranberries
    2 cups sugar
    ¼ cup fresh lemon juice

Combine the fruit with 2 cups water in a large saucepan. Bring the water to a boil and simmer the fruit, covered, for 15 to 20 minutes, or until the cranberries have all popped. Press the mixture through a fine sieve into a large bowl.

Heat the sugar with 4 cups water and the lemon juice in the saucepan over low heat, stirring until the sugar dissolves.

Into another saucepan ladle equal volumes of the cranberry purée and the sugar syrup and reheat the nectar over low heat until it comes to a boil.

Ladle the nectar into warm 1-pint jars and seal. Process in a boiling water bath for 15 minutes. Let cool completely before checking the seals and storing.

Makes 3 quarts

The kitchen garden at Hope End, Ledbury.

95

DRIED CRANBERRY TART WITH ALMOND CREAM

This tart makes a good winter dessert. Serve it with heavy cream or vanilla ice cream.

2 cups Dried Cranberries (page 93)
5 tablespoons kirsch
Basic Shortcrust Dough for one 12-inch
   tart (page 234)
6 tablespoons unsalted butter,
   softened
½ cup plus 2 tablespoons sugar
1 whole large egg, beaten
1 large egg yolk
1 cup blanched almonds, finely ground
2 tablespoons all-purpose flour
½ cup Apricot Jam (page 68)

Combine the dried cranberries with 4 tablespoons of the kirsch and let the fruit macerate for 1 hour.

Fit the dough into a 9- or 10-inch tart pan with a removable rim, prick the shell all over and chill for 30 to 45 minutes. Line the shell with foil, fill with pie weights or dried beans, and bake in a preheated 400° oven for 10 to 12 minutes, or until it is set and light golden. Remove the pie weights and set aside to cool. Turn the oven down to 350°.

Cream the butter, gradually beat in ½ cup of the sugar, and continue beating until the mixture is light and fluffy. Gradually add the whole egg and egg yolk, beating well. Add the remaining 1 tablespoon kirsch, stir in the almonds and flour, and spoon the almond cream into the shell.

Drain the cranberries, pat them dry, and arrange them on top of the almond cream.

Bake the tart in the 350° oven for 10 minutes. Sprinkle the top with the remaining 2 tablespoons sugar and continue baking until the almond cream is golden and firm to the touch. Let the tart cool in the pan on a wire rack. Remove the pan's rim and transfer the tart to a serving plate.

Strain the apricot jam through a sieve into a small saucepan and heat it over low heat until it is of spreading consistency. Brush the surface of the tart with the jam glaze and serve at room temperature.

Serves 6 to 8

RED CURRANT MAGIC

Mme Brassard, *directrice* of the Cordon Bleu Cooking School in Paris for forty years, let me in on this secret for making red currant jelly. Her no-cook method produces a very fresh fruit flavor and a crystal-clear substance. In France, red currant jelly is most often melted and used as a glaze for fresh red fruit tarts.

6 to 7 pounds red currants
About 4½ cups sugar

Purée the currants in a food processor and let them drain in a dampened jelly bag set over a large bowl for at least 12 hours or overnight.

Measure the strained juice and for every 2 cups of it measure 1½ cups of sugar. Combine the sugar and the juice in a preserving pan and stir the mixture vigorously with a wooden spoon until all the sugar is dissolved and the mixture is slightly stiffened. (Mme Brassard suggests working in the sun for best results, but they can be achieved under gloomy skies as well.)

Ladle the jelly into sterilized jars and seal. The jelly keeps in a cool, dark place for 6 months. For an extended shelf life store the jelly in the refrigerator.

Makes 2 quarts

PINK BLUSH

There is a famous white currant preserve in France, from the town of Bar-le-Duc, that features whole, seeded white currants suspending in a clear jelly made from the juice of the same fruit. The interesting detail to note is that traditionally the seeds are removed from the fruit with the tip of a goose quill. This classic preserve is the inspiration for the following recipe, which is not, however, so labor-intensive. The suspended red currants add an amusing pink blush.

4 pounds white currants
About 4 cups sugar
¼ cup fresh lemon juice
2 cups red currants, stalked and
    stemmed

Combine the white currants with 2 cups water in a preserving pan. Bring the water to a boil over low heat and simmer the fruit for 15 to 20 minutes, or until nearly all the currants have split open.

Tip the contents of the pan into a dampened jelly bag set over a large bowl and let it drain for at least 12 hours or overnight.

Measure the strained juice, reserving it, and for every 2 cups juice measure 1 cup sugar. In a preserving pan combine the sugar and the lemon juice and cook the mixture over very low heat, stirring, until the sugar melts. Bring the syrup to a boil over moderate heat and add the currant juice. Boil the mixture, skimming any froth that surfaces, for 5 minutes, or until the jellying point is reached. Let the jelly stand for 10 minutes.

Carefully stir in the red currants. Ladle the jelly into warm sterilized jars and seal.

Makes 2 quarts

*Vine-ripened red and
white currants at
Rodmarton Manor,
Gloucestershire.*

97

Tempting fruit jellies made from (clockwise, from top left) greengage plums, quince, and black currants.

BLACK CURRANT FRUIT JELLIES

Fruit jellies or fruit pastes (from the French *pâtes de fruits*) are candies of concentrated flavor made from the pulp of a fruit possessing a fair amount of sugar. For variations based on this technique, substitute an equal quantity of red currants, blackberries, or raspberries for the black currants. Other fruits well suited to this concentrated form are apricots, quinces, and plums.

3 pounds black currants
2 tablespoons fresh lemon juice
About 3 cups superfine sugar
Granulated sugar, for coating the
    candies

In a large bowl combine the black currants and lemon juice. Crush the fruit with the back of a wooden spoon. Let the fruit stand, covered, overnight.

Tip the contents of the bowl into a preserving pan, bring to a boil over low heat, and simmer for 15 to 20 minutes, or until the fruit is softened completely.

Force the fruit through a fine sieve into a bowl. Measure the purée and for every 2 cups purée measure 1 cup of superfine sugar. Return the purée to the pan and stir in the sugar. Cook the mixture over low heat, stirring frequently, until the sugar dissolves. Bring the mixture to a boil and boil it for about 30 minutes, or until it is very thick and easily comes away from the sides of the pan.

Rinse out a large rectangular baking pan, 10½ x 15½ x 1 inch, with cold water and shake it dry, leaving a few drops inside. Pour the fruit paste into the dish, smooth the surface, and let it stand, covered loosely with foil, overnight.

Turn the paste out onto a work surface sprinkled generously with granulated sugar. Cut the slab into approximately 1½-inch squares and toss the squares in more granulated sugar to coat them completely. Set the squares on a wire rack to dry for a few days and then store in an airtight container, separating the layers with wax paper.

Makes 2 dozen 1½-inch squares

CREME DE CASSIS

Crème de cassis is an alcohol-based black currant syrup. The most renowned use of this syrup is in the making of a Kir, an apéritif made with a splash of cassis blended with a white Aligoté wine from Burgundy. Traditionally cassis is made by steeping the currants in *eau-de-vie de marc*, which is a clear alcohol distilled from the lees left after pressing wine grapes. If *marc* is not available, substitute an Italian grappa, which is a similar spirit.

2 pounds black currants, plus 3 or 4
  black currant leaves
1 whole clove
3-inch cinnamon stick
2 cups sugar
2 pints *eau-de-vie de marc*

In a 2-quart jar, combine the black currants with the leaves, clove, cinnamon stick, sugar, and *eau-de-vie* and let the fruit macerate, turning the jar upside down occasionally during the first week to distribute the sugar, for 1 month.

Transfer the mixture to a fine sieve set over a bowl and press lightly on the solids. Strain the resulting liquid a second time through dampened cheesecloth into another bowl to ensure clarity. Ladle the syrup into attractive jars or bottles and store in a cool place.

Makes about 2 quarts

Black currants freshly gathered from wild roadside bushes.

FIG CREPES WITH
CHARTREUSE CUSTARD SAUCE

This dessert will make a very snappy ending to any meal. The whole preserved figs are wrapped in light, buttery crêpes and laced with a little Chartreuse. A generous dash of the liqueur is also added to the custard sauce. Despite its bright green color, Chartreuse is the only 100 percent natural French liqueur. The brandy-based drink is made from a secret blend of honey and herbs concocted by Carthusian monks.

6 large egg yolks
½ cup granulated sugar
2 cups milk, scalded
3 to 4 tablespoons Chartreuse
2 cups Fresh Fig and Vine-Ripened
   Grape Jam (page 104)
Crêpes (page 229)
2 tablespoons unsalted butter, cut into
   bits
2 tablespoons brown sugar

In a mixing bowl beat the egg yolks and sugar together until the mixture is thick and

pale. Gradually whisk the milk into the mixture. Transfer the custard to a saucepan and cook over low heat, stirring constantly for 7 to 8 minutes, or until the custard starts to thicken. Stir in 2 tablespoons of the Chartreuse, strain the custard into a small bowl or sauceboat, and cover the surface directly with plastic wrap.

Spoon some of the fig jam onto one of the crêpes and roll it into a loose cylinder or fold it in half twice, forming a triangle. Continue filling and folding crêpes in the same manner until all the crêpes and jam have been used. The recipe may be prepared up to this point in advance and kept, covered, for several hours.

Arrange the crêpes in a single layer in a buttered gratin dish. Sprinkle the crêpes with the remaining 1 or 2 tablespoons Chartreuse, dot them with the butter, and sprinkle them with the brown sugar. Bake the crêpes in a preheated 350° oven for 15 to 20 minutes, or until the topping is slightly caramelized. Serve with the custard sauce.

Serves 8 to 10

FRESH FIG AND
VINE-RIPENED GRAPE JAM

This jam is truly Provençal, in both spirit and substance. I first made it with the help of Richard Olney while visiting the south of France one September. At that time the vines sheltering his outdoor dining area were laden with intensely blue-black grapes (an old variety called Jaquet), and we were receiving a daily supply of small brown-skinned figs from Henri, a very obliging neighbor, in quantities larger than we cared to consume fresh. We decided to transform the ingredients into a jam based on the old regional method of using reduced grape juice as a substitute for sugar, a practice developed in times when sugar was scarce. Although the natural sugar content of grapes is extremely high, it is best to extend the shelf life of this preserve by processing the jars in a water bath.

> 5 to 5½ pounds small ripe figs
> 6 pounds grapes, preferably a red-wine variety (otherwise red table grapes will do)
> Several sprigs of fresh thyme

Remove any tough skin around the stem ends of the figs and set them aside.

Remove the grapes from the stalks and if you have the strength and patience, pass them directly through a sieve set over a bowl. Alternatively, crush the grapes in a food processor and strain the resulting pulp through a sieve.

Transfer the strained juice to a preserving pan and add the figs and thyme. Bring the mixture slowly to a boil, stirring occasionally, and boil it for 10 minutes. With a slotted spoon transfer the figs to a large sieve or colander set over a bowl.

Bring the juice in the pan back to a boil and boil it for 5 minutes to reduce it slightly. Return the figs and any collected juices to the preserving pan and cook them for another 10 minutes.

Repeat the transferring and reducing procedure until the figs are soft when pierced with the tip of a knife. Transfer the figs one last time to the sieve and continue reducing the juice until the jellying point is reached. Discard the thyme.

Divide the figs among warm jars. Cover the fruit with the syrup and seal the jars. Process the jars in a boiling water bath: 5 minutes for jars up to 1 pint, 10 minutes for jars up to 1 quart. Let the jars cool completely before checking the seals and storing.

Makes 3 quarts

RED GOOSEBERRY JELLY WITH ELDER FLOWERS

The sweet-smelling flowers of the elder blossom in early June, during the peak of gooseberry season, and they impart a distinctive flavor to this jelly.

5 pounds red gooseberries
About 4 cups sugar
¼ cup fresh lemon juice
10 to 12 elder flower heads

Combine the gooseberries with 2 cups water in a large saucepan and simmer gently for about 45 minutes, or until the fruit is very soft.

Tip the contents of the pan into a dampened jelly bag set over a large bowl and let it drain for at least 12 hours or overnight.

Measure the strained juice and for every 2 cups juice measure 1 cup sugar. Combine the juice and sugar with the lemon juice in a preserving pan. Slowly bring the juice to a boil over low heat, stirring to dissolve the sugar. Tie the elder flowers in a cheesecloth bag, add the bag to the juice mixture, and boil the mixture until the jellying point is reached.

Discard the flowers and ladle the jam into warm sterilized jars and seal.

Makes about 2 quarts

The end-of-the-season gooseberries at Rodmarton Manor, Gloucestershire.

GOOSEBERRY JUICE

Gooseberry juice is convenient to have in the freezer for making jams or jellies with a low-pectin fruit, such as rhubarb or strawberries. (Gooseberries are high in acid and pectin—the two essentials in setting a preserve.) Use 1 cup juice for every 1 pound of low-pectin fruit.

4 pounds gooseberries

Combine the gooseberries and 2 cups water in a heavy saucepan and slowly bring the liquid to a boil. Reduce the heat and simmer the berries for 15 minutes, or until they can be crushed against the side of the pan with a wooden spoon.

Transfer the mixture to a dampened jelly bag set over a large bowl and let it drain for at least 12 hours or overnight. Divide the juice among freezer containers.

Makes 1 quart

GOOSEBERRIES IN SYRUP

2 cups sugar
2 tablespoons fresh lemon juice
A large handful of elder flower heads
  (optional)
4 pounds gooseberries

Combine the sugar and 4 cups water in a heavy saucepan, and cook over low heat, stirring until the sugar is dissolved. Add the lemon juice and elder flowers, if using, simmer for 10 minutes, and let cool.

Meanwhile, trim both ends of the gooseberries if there are small stems and slightly nick the skins to prevent their shriveling during processing. Divide the gooseberries among three 1-quart jars.

Pour the cooled syrup over the berries and process the jars in a cold water bath for 10 minutes. Let the jars cool completely before checking the seals and storing.

Makes 3 quarts

GRILLED MACKEREL WITH GOOSEBERRIES

Grilled mackerel and tart gooseberries are often seen combined in classic French cuisine; it's not surprising when you discover that the French word for gooseberry is *groseille à maquereau*, or "mackerel currant." Serve the fish with boiled new potatoes.

Two ¾-pound whole mackerels,
  gutted and cleaned
6 tablespoons olive oil
Salt and freshly ground pepper
2 cups drained Gooseberries in Syrup
  (at left), plus ½ cup of the syrup
1 cup heavy cream
1 tablespoon dry mustard
¼ cup minced flat-leaf parsley

Rub the mackerels all over with the oil and season them lightly with salt and pepper. Cook the fish in a pan on an outdoor grill or under a preheated broiler for 10 minutes. Turn the fish carefully and add the gooseberries to the pan. Cook the fish for 10 minutes more, or until they are hot in the center when pierced with a skewer. Carefully turn the gooseberries from time to time to heat them through.

Meanwhile, in a small saucepan boil the ½ cup gooseberry syrup until it is reduced to 2 tablespoons. Stir in the cream and mustard and boil the mixture until it is slightly reduced. Add the parsley and season the sauce with salt and pepper to taste.

Split and bone each whole mackerel into 2 servings and serve them with the grilled gooseberries and sauce.

Serves 4

*Grilled Mackerel with
Gooseberries.*

GRAPES IN GRAPE JUICE

The quality of bottled grapes should not be underestimated. When preserved by the cold-pack method (see Bottling, page 19), the fruit remains firm and succulent. The grapes are delicious as fillings for tarts (such as Walnut and Grape Tart, page 112).

8 pounds black or green seedless
    grapes
3 cups sugar
2 tablespoons fresh lemon juice

Crush 4 pounds of the grapes in a food processor until they are nearly completely liquified. Strain the juice through a sieve lined with dampened cheesecloth set over a bowl. There should be at least 3 cups juice.

In a large saucepan, combine the strained juice with the sugar, lemon juice, and 3 cups water and heat the mixture over low heat, stirring until the sugar is dissolved. Increase the heat, boil the mixture for 5 minutes, and set it aside to cool. Meanwhile, divide the remaining grapes among four 1-quart jars.

When the syrup is cooled, pour enough into each jar to reach the capacity level. Process the jars in a cold water bath for 10 minutes. Let the jars cool completely before testing the seals and storing.

Makes 4 quarts

The well-groomed greenhouse at Stowell Park, Gloucestershire, with Lady Downe's Seedling grapes.

GUAVA HONEY

This confection is nice for spreading on warm scones and as a filling for meringues, cakes, or Tropical Triangles (at right).

    2½ pounds guavas, unpeeled, stem
        ends trimmed off
    ¼ cup fresh lime juice
    2 cups honey, such as acacia or orange
        blossom

Thinly slice the guavas and in a preserving pan combine them with the lime juice and ¼ cup water. Bring the mixture to a boil over low heat and simmer it for 20 minutes, or until the fruit is softened and nearly all the liquid is evaporated.

Strain the mixture through a fine sieve set over a bowl and discard the seeds. Wipe out the preserving pan; in it combine the strained pulp and the honey, and bring the mixture to a boil.

Ladle the honey into small warm jars and seal. Process the jars in a boiling water bath for 5 minutes. Let the jars cool completely before checking the seals and storing.

Makes 2½ cups

GUAVA JELLY

I would only recommend making this jelly if you can obtain very fresh guavas. The flavor and perfumelike aroma of these fragile little fruits is very transient.

    4 pounds guavas, unpeeled, stem ends
        trimmed off
    About 1½ cups sugar
    1 tablespoon fresh lemon juice

Thinly slice the guavas and in a preserving pan combine them with 4 cups water, or enough to barely cover the fruit. Bring the water to a boil and simmer the fruit for 45 minutes, or until it can be easily crushed against the side of the pan with a wooden spoon.

Tip the contents of the pan into a dampened jelly bag set over a large bowl and let it drain for at least 12 hours or overnight.

Measure the strained juice and for every 1 cup of it measure ½ cup of sugar. In the preserving pan combine the sugar and juice and cook the mixture over moderate heat, stirring, until the sugar dissolves. Add the lemon juice, bring the mixture to a boil, and boil it, skimming the jelly, for 10 minutes, or until the jellying point is reached.

Ladle the jelly into warm sterilized jars and seal.

Makes 1 quart

TROPICAL TRIANGLES

The guava honey filling makes this recipe quite special. Other tropical fruit spreads, such as Mango Butter (page 120) or Passion Fruit Curd (page 131) would be equally good fillings.

    1 cup all-purpose flour
    Salt
    ¼ teaspoon freshly grated lemon zest
    ¼ cup light brown sugar
    ⅓ cup cold unsalted butter, cut into
        bits
    2 large eggs, separated
    ¼ cup granulated sugar
    ⅓ cup whole blanched almonds,
        toasted, cooled, and finely ground
    ½ cup Guava Honey (at left)
    Confectioners' sugar, for dusting

In a bowl combine the flour, a pinch of salt, the zest, and brown sugar. Rub the butter into the mixture with your fingertips until it is dispersed uniformly. In a small bowl beat the yolks and stir them gently into the crumb mixture with a fork until the mixture is just combined.

Press the crumb mixture gently into a buttered 8-inch square baking pan. Bake it in a preheated 350° oven for 8 to 10 minutes, or until it is golden, and let it cool in the pan on a rack. Reduce the oven temperature to 325°.

Beat the egg whites with a pinch of salt until soft peaks form. Gradually beat in the granulated sugar, beating until the meringue is stiff and glossy. Carefully fold in the almonds.

Spread the guava honey over the crust, leaving a ¼-inch border on all sides, and over it spread the meringue. Bake for 20 to 25 minutes, or until the meringue is lightly golden, and let it cool in the pan on a rack.

When the pan is cool enough to touch, sprinkle the meringue with a light coating of the confectioners' sugar. Slice the bars into sixteen 2-inch squares and slice each square in half to make 2 triangles.

Makes 32 triangles

KUMQUATS IN BRANDY SYRUP

Kumquats are closely related to the citrus family, having an acidic juice yet sweet rind. The whole fruit—flesh, seeds, and peel—is edible, particularly when steeped in a brandy syrup for a couple of months. In England kumquats are associated with Christmas and are often served as an element of afternoon tea.

    1½ pounds firm unblemished
      kumquats
    ¾ cup sugar
    1 vanilla bean, split lengthwise
    3 cups brandy

Wash the kumquats well. In a saucepan blanch them in boiling water for 1 minute and drain them. Let the kumquats cool and prick them a few times each with a needle (this keeps them from bursting open during further cooking).

In a saucepan combine the sugar with 2 cups water, bring to a boil over low heat, stirring, until the sugar is dissolved. Add the vanilla bean and simmer the syrup for 10 minutes. Add the kumquats to the syrup, bring the syrup back to a boil, and simmer them for 5 minutes.

Transfer the kumquats to a warm 1½-quart jar with a slotted spoon. Reduce the syrup over moderate heat until only 1 cup remains, let it cool, and remove the vanilla bean, reserving it if desired.

Stir the brandy into the cooled syrup and pour the mixture over the fruit. (If you like, add the vanilla bean.) Store the unopened jar in a cool, dark place for a few weeks before eating.

Makes 1½ quarts

PRESERVED LEMONS

Lemons preserved in brine can be purchased in specialty foods shops, but they are extremely simple to prepare at home. Use them as a flavoring for stews, an accompaniment to grilled fish, or as an hors d'oeuvre served thinly sliced, drizzled with olive oil, and sprinkled with chopped fresh mint and black pepper. The lemons need at least 4 to 6 weeks to absorb the salt and change character. Once the jar is opened, any remaining lemons will keep, chilled, for several months.

4 very firm medium lemons (about
    6 ounces each)
⅓ cup fine sea salt
3-inch cinnamon stick
2 teaspoons coriander seeds
1 teaspoon black peppercorns
4 whole cloves

Bring a large saucepan of water to a boil and add the lemons. Return the water to a boil, boil the lemons for 3 minutes, and transfer them with a slotted spoon to a bowl of cold water. When the lemons are cool enough to handle, drain them and pat them dry.

In another saucepan combine 3 cups water with the salt, cinnamon stick, coriander seeds, peppercorns, and cloves and bring the mixture to a boil. Set aside.

Stand each lemon upright and cut it into quarters, leaving the quarters attached at the base. Pack the lemons tightly into a warm sterilized 1½-quart jar and pour the boiling-hot spice mixture over the lemons to cover. Tuck the cinnamon stick into the jar and seal.

Makes 1½ quarts

*Whole Preserved Lemons
are not only eye-catching
in appearance, but are
marvelously versatile in
their use.*

116

LAMB SHANKS WITH EGGPLANT AND PRESERVED LEMONS

The preserved lemons add a Moroccan touch to this basic ragout. The flavors of the dish actually improve if it is prepared at least one day in advance, which makes this a perfect dish for entertaining. Rice pilaf or pasta make the best accompaniments for the shanks and sauce.

3 tablespoons all-purpose flour
1 teaspoon sweet Hungarian paprika
3 to 3½ pounds lamb shanks, trimmed
6 tablespoons extra-virgin olive oil
½ cup dry white wine
8 garlic cloves, unpeeled
1 pound eggplant, preferably long and
   narrow
1 Preserved Lemon (page 116),
   quartered and cut crosswise into
   ¼-inch slices
½ cup minced flat-leaf parsley
Salt and freshly ground pepper

Over a piece of foil on a large plate sift together the flour and paprika. Dredge the lamb shanks lightly in the mixture.

In a large skillet heat 2 tablespoons of the oil over moderately high heat. Add the shanks, in batches if necessary, brown them all over, and transfer them to another plate, lined with paper towels, to drain. Put the shanks in an ovenproof casserole.

Pour off any excess oil from the skillet, add the wine, and bring it to a boil over high heat, stirring and scraping up any browned bits. Strain the sauce over the lamb shanks. Wipe out the skillet.

Add the garlic to the casserole and bake the lamb, basting it every 15 minutes, in a preheated 350° oven for about 1¼ hours, or until it is tender.

While the lamb is cooking, halve the eggplant lengthwise and cut it crosswise into ½-inch pieces. In the skillet heat 2 tablespoons of the oil over high heat until it is very hot but not smoking and in it sauté half the eggplant, for 3 to 4 minutes on each side, or until it is browned. Transfer the eggplant to a plate, lined with paper towels, to drain. Repeat the procedure with the remaining eggplant and oil.

Add the eggplant and the lemons to the lamb and bake the mixture for 15 minutes longer. Add the parsley and salt and pepper to taste. The ragout may be made 1 day in advance and reheated, in which case add the parsley only after the reheating.

Serves 4

LEMON OR LIME CURD

Fruit curds are made with fruit juices or purées with the addition of egg yolks and butter, and it is these last—the dairy products—that limit the curds' shelf life. They should thus be consumed within a few months of being made. Lemon curd is generally used as a filling in a pre-baked tart shell, a jelly roll, or a sponge layer cake.

6 large egg yolks
1 cup superfine sugar
¾ cup fresh lemon or lime juice (from
   4 lemons or 8 limes)
Grated zest of 4 lemons or 4 limes
1 stick (½ cup) unsalted butter, cut
   into bits

In a double boiler over simmering water beat the egg yolks and sugar together until the mixture is thick and very pale.

Beat in the juice and grated zest. Gradually stir in the butter and continue to cook, stirring constantly, for about 20 minutes, or until very thick. (Do not let the mixture boil or the eggs will curdle.)

Spoon the curd into sterilized jars and seal. The curd keeps, unopened and chilled, for 2 to 3 months.

Makes 1 quart

LYCHEES IN LIME SYRUP

Home-preserved lychees bear no resemblance to the familiar dessert seen far too frequently in modest Chinese restaurants. In this recipe the fruit keeps its fresh natural taste, which is enhanced by the blend of limes and dried linden leaves.

  ½ cup dried linden leaves
  2 cups sugar
  1 pound limes
  4 pounds fresh lychees, peeled and
    pitted

Bring 4 cups water to a boil in a large preserving pan. Remove from the heat, stir in the linden leaves and sugar, and let the mixture stand, covered, for 30 minutes.

Meanwhile blanch the limes in a large saucepan of boiling water for 1 minute, drain them, and let them cool until they can be handled easily. Slice the limes very thin.

Skim off and discard as many of the linden leaves as possible (it doesn't matter if some stay in). Add the lychees and lime slices to the sugar syrup and bring the liquid just to a boil.

Divide the lychees and limes among four warm 1-quart jars with a slotted spoon and pour enough syrup into each jar to cover the fruit. Seal the jars and process them in a boiling water bath for 20 minutes. Let the jars cool completely before checking the seals and storing.

Makes 4 quarts

CLEMENTINES IN BLOOD ORANGE SYRUP

These clementines make a perfect ending to any meal. Serve them plain with their syrup, or with a custard sauce, garnished with candied orange rind.

2 cups blood orange juice, fresh (about
    6 oranges) or frozen (at right),
    thawed
4 cups sugar
3-inch cinnamon stick
5 whole cloves
2 cardamom pods
6 pounds clementines or mandarins,
    peeled
¼ cup orange liqueur, if desired

In a large saucepan combine the blood orange juice, 6 cups water, and the sugar and heat the mixture over low heat, stirring, until the sugar is dissolved. Tie the spices in a small piece of cheesecloth and add them to the sugar syrup. Boil the mixture for 5 minutes to impart the flavors.

Add the clementines to the syrup and simmer them for 10 minutes. Remove the pan from the heat and let the fruit mixture stand, covered, overnight.

Slowly bring the liquid back to a boil. Transfer the fruit with a slotted spoon to 3 warm 1-quart jars. Remove the spice bag and boil the liquid for 10 minutes to reduce slightly. Add the liqueur to the syrup.

Divide the hot syrup among the jars, seal the jars, and process in a boiling water bath for 15 minutes. Let the jars cool completely before checking the seals and storing.

Makes 3 quarts

The colors of Whole Clementines in Blood Orange Syrup make them particularly festive for a Christmastime dessert.

BLOOD ORANGE JUICE

The tart, deep-red juice of the blood orange makes a wonderful addition to sauces.

12 blood oranges

Cut the oranges in half, extract the juice and strain it. Pour the juice into ice cube trays, about 2 tablespoons per cube, and freeze it. Transfer the cubes to freezer bags and store them for up to 6 months.

Makes 3 cups

MALTAISE SAUCE

This orange-flavored hollandaise sauce makes a perfect accompaniment to grilled fish or fresh asparagus.

3 tablespoons white wine vinegar
½ teaspoon salt
3 large egg yolks, lightly beaten
2 sticks (1 cup) unsalted butter, cut
    into bits
Pinch of cayenne pepper
¼ cup blood orange juice, fresh or
    frozen (above), thawed

In a small heavy nonreactive saucepan combine the vinegar, 1 tablespoon water, and the salt and reduce the liquid by half over moderate heat.

Over low heat stir in 1 tablespoon cold water, whisk in the yolks, and cook the mixture, stirring, until it has thickened slightly. Whisk in the butter, a few bits at a time—be prepared to take the pan off the heat from time to time as overheating will curdle the eggs—and continue whisking until the sauce is very thick. Add the cayenne and the juice and taste for seasoning.

Keep the sauce warm in a hot water bath.

Makes 1½ cups

PLAIN ORANGE CURD

Orange curd is best spread on warm muffins or used as a filling for precooked tart shells, or as part of Orange Curd and Chocolate Tart (at right).

2 medium oranges
1 large lemon
2 large whole eggs plus 2 large egg
   yolks
¾ cup sugar
6 tablespoons unsalted butter, cut into
   bits

Scrub the oranges and lemon thoroughly and dry them well. Grate the zest and squeeze the juice from the fruit into a bowl.

In a double boiler set over simmering water beat the whole eggs and yolks until they are pale. Gradually beat in the sugar and continue beating the mixture over the heat until it is thickened.

Stir in the juice, zest, and butter, stirring until the butter is melted and the mixture is thick enough to coat the back of a wooden spoon. (Do not let the mixture boil or the eggs will curdle.)

Ladle the curd into small sterilized jars and seal. The curd keeps, unopened and chilled, for 2 to 3 months.

Makes 3 cups

ORANGE CURD AND CHOCOLATE TART

A tart shell flavored with toasted walnuts and coated with bittersweet chocolate makes a delicious and elegant container for the orange curd filling.

1 cup all-purpose flour
½ cup walnuts, toasted, cooled, and
   finely ground
2 tablespoons sugar
Pinch of salt
5 tablespoons unsalted butter, cut into
   bits
3 ounces bittersweet chocolate
1½ cups Plain Orange Curd (at left)
Unsweetened cocoa powder, for
   dusting

In a bowl combine the flour, nuts, sugar, and salt and work in the butter with your fingertips until the mixture resembles coarse meal. Add 3 to 4 tablespoons ice-cold water, or just enough to form the dough into a ball. Chill the dough, wrapped in plastic wrap or wax paper, for 30 minutes.

Roll the dough into a 12-inch round on a lightly floured surface. Fit the dough into a 10-inch tart pan with a removable rim, prick the dough all over and chill for 30 minutes.

Line the shell with foil, and fill with pie weights or dried beans, and bake in a preheated 425° oven for 10 minutes. Remove the foil and weights, and continue baking the crust for 5 to 7 minutes, or until it is golden. Let the crust cool in the pan on a rack.

In a double boiler melt the chocolate over simmering water. Spread the melted chocolate on the bottom of the shell. Let the chocolate set. Spoon the orange curd over the set chocolate, smoothing the surface. Dust the tart with cocoa powder. Transfer the tart from the pan to a serving plate.

Makes one 10-inch tart

DARK BITTER ORANGE AND GINGER MARMALADE

Seville oranges are a bitter-tasting fruit and are generally reserved for cooking purposes rather than eating out of hand. They are available only seasonally, so if you would like to have a supply throughout the year it is worthwhile to make several batches of marmalade at a time.

3 pounds Seville oranges, scrubbed well
2 medium lemons, scrubbed well
2½ cups granulated sugar
2 cups firmly packed light brown sugar
¼ cup minced preserved stem ginger

Combine the oranges and lemons with 1½ quarts water in a large saucepan. Bring the water to a boil over low heat and simmer the fruit, covered, for about 1½ hours, or until it is very tender when pierced with a skewer. Drain the fruit, in a colander set over a bowl, reserving the cooking liquid, and let the fruit cool.

Chop or slice the fruit, unpeeled, into the desired texture, reserving the seeds. Tie the seeds in a piece of cheesecloth.

Return the liquid in the bowl to the pan, add the granulated and brown sugars, and cook the mixture over low heat, stirring, until the sugar is dissolved. Bring the sugar syrup to a boil, add the prepared fruit and bag of seeds, and boil the mixture, stirring frequently and skimming the froth, for about 30 minutes, or until the jellying point is reached.

Stir in the ginger, ladle the marmalade into warm sterilized jars, and seal.

Makes 4 quarts

Antique marmalade jars make amusing containers for homemade preserves.

Three different stages of the Gâteau Léger au Chocolat: a plain layer of chocolate cake, a layer covered with slices of preserved blood oranges, and a layer with blood oranges and chocolate mousse.

GATEAU LEGER AU CHOCOLAT

The recipe for this cake comes from Dominique Bouchet, former chef at the Tour d'Argent in Paris. The method is nearly foolproof, provided that the very best chocolate available is used. Although the minted oranges are not part of the original "formula," I think that they are a respectable addition.

3 large eggs
⅓ cup sugar
¼ cup all-purpose flour
¼ cup unsweetened cocoa powder
   plus additional for dusting
3 tablespoons unsalted butter, melted
   and cooled
2 cups drained Blood Oranges in Fresh
   Mint Syrup plus additional if desired
   (page 129)
8 ounces good-quality bittersweet
   chocolate
2 cups heavy cream

In a large heatproof bowl with an electric mixer beat the eggs until they are thick and pale. Gradually beat in the sugar. Set the bowl over a saucepan of hot water and beat the mixture until it has increased considerably in volume and is very thick. Remove the bowl from the pan and continue to beat the mixture until it is cooled.

Sift the flour and the ¼ cup cocoa powder together and fold the mixture into the egg mixture alternately with the butter. Pour the batter into a buttered and floured 10-inch round cake pan and bake the cake in a preheated 350° oven for 25 to 30 minutes, or until it shrinks slightly from the sides of the pan. Let the cake cool for about 10 minutes in the pan on a rack and invert it onto the rack to cool completely.

Slice the cake in half horizontally and trim one of the halves to fit inside an 8-inch round springform pan, reserving the other half for another use. Place the trimmed cake, cut-side up, inside the springform pan. Brush the mint syrup from the oranges over the surface and arrange the oranges on top. Set the cake aside.

In a double boiler melt the chocolate over simmering water, stirring. In a large bowl whip the cream until soft peaks form and pour the hot chocolate over it in a steady stream, whisking until the mousse mixture is just combined.

Pour the chocolate mousse over the oranges, smooth the top, and chill the cake for at least 8 hours or overnight.

To serve, remove the cake from the springform pan, dust with cocoa powder and slice it into thin wedges. Serve with additional oranges in syrup if you like.

Serves 8 to 10

DRIED ORANGE PEEL

Drying orange peel is a simple and quick operation. During the drying process the flavors of the oils in the peel become concentrated, and they can impart a delicate taste to both sweet and savory dishes. For example, a 2-inch piece of dried peel can be added to beef or veal stews or it can be ground with sugar in a food processor or spice grinder and used to flavor cakes and cookies.

The best flavor is derived from Seville or blood oranges, although more ordinary varieties are perfectly suitable.

Thoroughly scrub the fruit and pat it dry. Remove the peel with a sharp paring knife or vegetable peeler. (Do not include the white pith, which has a bitter taste.)

Thread a trussing needle with string and thread the strips, leaving airing space between them. Hang the threaded peels in a warm room and let them dry for 3 to 4 days, or until they are shriveled. The peel keeps in a well-sealed jar for up to 1 year.

BLOOD ORANGES IN FRESH MINT SYRUP

Blood oranges start to appear in the market about March. Because they are available fresh for only a very limited period, it is wise to preserve them in some form to prolong the pleasure of their company. These minted oranges are very refreshing served on their own, or they can be used as a filling for Gâteau Léger au Chocolat (page 128).

5 pounds firm blood oranges
2½ cups clear white rock sugar
1 cup fresh mint leaves, blanched and
　patted dry

Remove the peel from the oranges, reserving the peel for drying (see Dried Orange Peel at left). Working over a large bowl to catch the juice, slice the oranges into ¼-inch rounds, discarding the seeds. Reserve the slices and juice in the bowl until all the oranges are sliced.

In a sterilized 1½-quart jar pack the orange slices in alternate layers with the sugar and mint. Chill the orange mixture for at least 1 week. Once opened, the oranges keep, chilled, for 4 to 6 weeks.

Makes 1½ quarts

PASSION FRUIT CURD

This curd can be used as a filling for tartlets or as a dessert sauce if thinned with a little heavy cream.

  2 pounds passion fruit
  Grated zest and juice of 1 lime
  1 cup superfine sugar
  1 stick (½ cup) unsalted butter, cut
     into bits
  4 large eggs, lightly beaten

Extract the juice and seeds from the passion fruit and strain out the seeds. In a double boiler or a heavy saucepan whisk the passion fruit juice with the lime zest and juice, sugar, butter, and eggs.

Cook the mixture over simmering water or low heat, stirring constantly, for about 30 minutes, or until the sugar is dissolved and the mixture is thickened. (Do not let the mixture boil or the eggs will curdle.)

Spoon the curd into sterilized jars and seal. The curd keeps, unopened and chilled, for 2 to 3 months. For longer storage, process the jars in a boiling water bath: 10 minutes for 1-pint jars, 15 minutes for 1-quart jars.

Makes 1 quart

WHOLE PRESERVED PEACHES WITH PISTACHIO CREAM

The Whole Apricots in Vanilla Syrup (page 69) can be used in place of the peaches in this recipe. To get the best pistachio flavor, use dark green nuts; the yellow nuts indicate old age.

  2 cups shelled pistachios
  4 Whole Peaches in Almond Syrup
     (page 133), plus ¼ cup of the syrup
  1½ cups milk
  5 large egg yolks

  ¼ cup sugar
  Fresh mint or lemon leaves, for garnish

Drop the nuts into a pan of boiling water and blanch for 1 minute. Drain the pistachios and vigorously rub them in a tea towel to remove the skins. Peel stubborn nuts with your fingers.

Drain the preserved peaches and set them aside with the ¼ cup syrup. Finely chop 1½ cups of the pistachios, reserving the remaining ½ cup for garnish.

In a small saucepan combine the chopped pistachios with the milk, bring the milk to a boil, and let the mixture stand off the heat, covered, for 1 hour.

While the pistachio mixture is standing, in a small bowl whisk together the egg yolks and sugar until the mixture is thick and pale.

Heat the pistachio mixture over low heat until the milk is scalded, strain it into a bowl, and discard the pistachios. Gradually whisk the milk into the yolks, return the mixture to the saucepan, and heat it gently, stirring constantly, until the custard is thick and coats the back of a wooden spoon. Cover the surface of the pistachio cream with a piece of wax paper until ready to serve.

Spoon the pistachio cream into a large shallow serving dish or individual plates, arrange the peaches on top, and drizzle them with the reserved syrup. Coarsely chop the reserved ½ cup pistachios and sprinkle them over the peaches. Garnish the desserts with the mint leaves.

Serves 4

Whole Preserved Peaches with Pistachio Cream can be enjoyed with a sweet wine, such as a Sauternes.

WHOLE PEACHES IN ALMOND SYRUP

If you prefer your preserved peaches halved rather than whole (they do fit the jars more easily as halves), halve them once the skins have been removed and discard the pits.

6 pounds small ripe peaches, preferably freestones
4 cups sugar
¼ cup almond-flavored liqueur

Immerse the peaches in a large pan of boiling water for 30 seconds, or until the skins seem loose enough to be easily peeled off, and drain them in a colander. Peel the peaches while they are still hot. Cut 2 or 3 peaches in half to extract the kernels from their pits.

In a large saucepan combine 2 quarts water with the sugar and peach kernels and heat the mixture over low heat, stirring until the sugar is dissolved. Bring the syrup to a boil and simmer the peaches in batches in the syrup for 10 minutes, transferring them to six warm 1-quart jars as they are done.

Boil the syrup for 10 minutes more to reduce it slightly. Remove the peach kernels and stir in the liqueur. Pour the almond syrup over the fruit, seal the jars and process them in a boiling water bath for 20 minutes. Let the jars cool completely before checking the seals and storing.

Makes 6 quarts

At Stowell Park
in Gloucestershire,
the greenhouse boasts a
healthy crop of nectarines
and peaches.

133

MOLDED PEACH "CHEESE"

Fruit cheeses are made by cooking a high proportion of sugar to fruit pulp until the excess moisture evaporates and the fruit is nearly stiff enough to keep a wooden spoon standing upright. In addition to peaches and nectarines, plums, quinces, and soft red fruits are often treated in a similar way. In fact, this preserving method appears in the confections of many countries. In England molded damson cheese is a Christmas specialty, and it is often served with cream cheese, nuts, and a glass of Sherry or Port. In Spain and Italy a quince "paste" is popular, and it is normally shaped into a rectangular slab from which chunks can be sliced. In France this paste, called *pâte de fruits,* is made into thick squares that are a popular after-school treat for children (see Black Currant Fruit Jellies, page 98). Fruit "leathers," available in the United States, are another form of this fruit mixture: The cooked fruit is spread in a thin layer onto a sheet of plastic wrap and rolled into convenient cylinders when dried. Apricot and strawberry seem to be the most popular fruit leathers. Experiment with a combination of flavors, such as quince and apple or cranberry and apple.

3 pounds firm-ripe peaches
¼ cup fresh lemon juice
About 1½ pounds (about 3 cups) sugar
2 teaspoons finely grated fresh ginger

Thinly slice the peaches and drop the slices into a preserving pan containing the lemon juice and ¾ cup water. Crack 3 or 4 peach pits, remove the kernels, tie them in a cheesecloth bag, and add it to the pan.

Bring the water to a boil over low heat and simmer the peaches for 20 to 25 minutes, or until they are very soft and can be easily crushed against the side of the pan with a wooden spoon.

Discard the bag of peach kernels and transfer the peaches to a food processor or blender. (Wipe out the preserving pan in readiness for the final cooking.) Purée the peaches to a smooth consistency. As an extra refinement, you may wish to pass the purée through a fine sieve into a bowl.

Weigh the purée (be sure not to weigh the bowl) and return it to the pan. Calculate three-fourths of the weight of the fruit purée, weigh out this amount in sugar, and add the sugar to the purée.

Cook the mixture over low heat, stirring constantly, until the sugar is dissolved. Increase the heat, and boil the "cheese," stirring vigorously to prevent the sugar from sticking, for 20 to 25 minutes, or until the mixture is thick enough to separate on the bottom of the pan when a spoon is drawn across it. Remove the pan from the heat and stir in the ginger.

Brush a 4-cup decorative mold with a flavorless vegetable oil and pack the "cheese" into the form, being sure to reach all the decorative curves. Press a piece of plastic wrap on the surface and let the "cheese" cool.

To serve, dip the mold into a sink or large bowl of boiling-hot water for 2 to 3 minutes and invert it onto a platter. Slice the "cheese" into wedges and serve with a red fruit sauce and whipped cream. Or cut it into small cubes and serve it as an after-dinner sweet with coffee. The "cheese" keeps, tightly covered with foil and chilled, for 1 year.

Makes 4 cups

Molded Peach "Cheese" takes its decorative shape from a traditional English pudding mold.

PEACHES AND RASPBERRY CREAM

This is a good example of how quickly a preserve can be transformed into an elegant dessert.

4 Whole Peaches in Almond Syrup
  (page 133), plus 1 cup of the syrup
1 cup heavy cream
¾ cup Raspberry Purée (page 151)
¼ cup sliced almonds, toasted
Fresh mint sprigs, for garnish

Halve the preserved peaches, discarding the pits. Arrange 2 halves, cut-sides up, on each of 4 dessert plates.

In a bowl beat the cream until soft peaks form. Add ¼ cup of the raspberry purée to the whipped cream and beat until soft peaks form again. In another bowl combine the remaining ½ cup purée with the reserved almond syrup until the sauce is blended well.

Spoon a few tablespoons of the sauce around each serving of peaches and put a dollop of the raspberry cream in each peach half. Sprinkle the desserts with the almonds and garnish with the mint. Pass any remaining raspberry cream and sauce separately.

Serves 4

BEAUJOLAIS PEARS WITH CASSIS AND PRUNES

Pears in red wine are always striking to look at and delicious to eat—whether freshly poached or preserved in jars. In fact, it is difficult to discern the difference between the preserved pears made from the following recipe and freshly poached ones. Try to select pears of uniform size in order both to economize on space when packing them into the jars as well as to make a more attractive presentation.

4 bottles (750 ml each) Beaujolais
4 cups sugar
12 pounds firm-ripe pears, such as
  Bartlett or Comice
3-inch cinnamon stick
5 whole cloves
3 allspice berries
1 or 2 sprigs of fresh rosemary
36 prunes
⅓ cup *crème de cassis*

In a large nonreactive pan combine the wine and sugar, bring the mixture slowly to a boil, stirring occasionally until the sugar is dissolved, and remove from the heat.

Peel the pears, removing the blossom ends but leaving the stems intact. Drop the pears directly into the wine syrup to prevent discoloration.

Tie the cinnamon stick, broken in half, the cloves, and allspice in a square of cheesecloth. Add the spice bag, rosemary, and prunes to the syrup, bring the syrup slowly back to a boil, and simmer the pears for 20 minutes. (Note that the pears do not have to be completely cooked at this point.)

Discard the spice bag and rosemary and with a slotted spoon transfer the pears and prunes to large (2- or 3-quart) warm jars, standing the pears upright on the bottom layer and arranging the next layer of pears upside down. Continue alternating the pattern until the jars are filled.

Boil the syrup until it is reduced by about three-fourths, or the equivalent of 1 bottle of wine. Stir the *crème de cassis* into the syrup. Strain the liquid through a double thickness of dampened cheesecloth, ladle it into the jars, and seal the jars.

Process the jars in a boiling water bath: 1 hour for 2-quart jars, 1 hour and 10 minutes for 3-quart jars. Let them cool completely before checking the seals and storing.

Makes 6 quarts

Beaujolais Pears with Cassis and Prunes served with dollops of crème fraîche.

DUCK RAGOUT WITH BLACK-CURRANT PEARS

Serve this ragout with steamed potatoes or fresh noodles.

> 5-pound duck, cut into 6 serving
>   pieces, excess fat discarded
> 2 to 3 tablespoons flour
> 4 tablespoons olive oil
> 8 Poached Pears in Black Currant
>   Vinegar Syrup (page 141), plus ¼
>   cup syrup
> 1 onion, thinly sliced
> 1 carrot, thinly sliced
> Salt and freshly ground pepper
> 1 cup chicken stock or water
> 1 Bouquet Garni (page 237)
> 2 tablespoons unsalted butter

Preserved pears in a vinegar syrup are combined with jointed duck pieces to make a simple ragout.

Dust the duck pieces lightly with the flour. In a large sauté pan heat 2 tablespoons of the oil over moderately high heat until it is hot but not smoking and in it brown the duck. Transfer the duck to a plate. Pour the fat from the pan and blot any excess fat still in the pan with a paper towel, leaving all the browned bits. Add the ¼ cup vinegar syrup and deglaze the pan over high heat, stirring, until the syrup is reduced by half. Pour over the duck pieces.

Heat the remaining 2 tablespoons oil in the sauté pan and in it brown the onion and carrot. Season the vegetables lightly with salt and pepper. Add the stock and the bouquet garni and return the duck and any juices that have collected on the plate to the pan. Bring the liquid to a boil and simmer the mixture, covered, for 30 minutes.

Remove the duck breasts and set them aside. Continue cooking the remaining pieces for 20 to 30 minutes, or until they are very tender.

Meanwhile, once the breasts are cool enough to handle, remove the bones and slice each one lengthwise into 3 or 4 pieces. Transfer the sliced breast meat to a shallow baking dish. Add the 8 pear halves.

When the rest of the duck is tender, add it to the baking dish. Whisk the butter into the cooking liquid and then strain it over the duck. The ragout may be prepared up to this point 1 day in advance and reheated in the oven before serving. To serve immediately, heat the ragout in a preheated 350° oven for 10 minutes, or until the pears are warmed through.

Serves 4

SECKEL PEARS
IN MAPLE SYRUP

These preserved pears can be used as a filling for tarts and tortes or can simply be reheated in their syrup and served with fresh cream. If the pears are served baked, baste them with the syrup until a rich glaze is formed.

2 cups firmly packed light brown sugar
2 tablespoons fresh lemon juice
1 cup pure maple syrup
6 pounds seckel pears

In a large saucepan combine the brown sugar with 5 cups water and the lemon juice and cook the mixture over low heat, stirring, until the sugar is dissolved. Stir in the maple syrup.

Peel the pears, leaving the stems intact, and with a slotted spoon lower them into the sweet syrup. Bring the liquid to a boil and simmer the pears for 5 minutes.

Transfer the pears to warm 1-quart jars, alternating the direction of the pears.

Heat the syrup over moderately high heat until it is reduced by about ¼ cup and pour it over the pears and seal the jars. Process the jars in a boiling water bath for 20 minutes. Let the jars cool completely before checking the seals and storing.

Makes 3 quarts

CHUNKY VANILLA PEAR JAM

This jam is sweetened by the natural sugars in the pears and fruit juice. No additional sugar is required. The jam is good as a base for fruit tarts or spread on toasted slices of pound cake.

5 pounds pears, preferably Bartlett
Grated zest of 1 lemon
2 tablespoons fresh lemon juice
2 quarts unsweetened apple juice or
    white grape juice
1 vanilla bean, split lengthwise

Peel, quarter, and core the pears. Chop the pears into small cubes and toss them in a bowl with the lemon zest and juice. Set aside.

In a preserving pan combine the apple juice with the vanilla bean and reduce it by half over moderate heat. Remove the vanilla bean from the reduced juice and add the pears and their liquid. Bring the mixture to a boil over moderate heat and cook it, stirring frequently, for 30 to 40 minutes, or until the jellying point is reached.

Spoon the jam into warm sterilized jars and seal.

Makes 1½ quarts

A bumper crop of pears presents the opportunity to make a variety of preserves: poached whole in a syrup, or in jams and chutneys.

Overleaf: Greengage and Victoria plums, with the pastures of County Durham in the background.

PECAN TORTE WITH MAPLE PEARS

2 cups whole pecans, toasted and
    cooled, plus 1 cup finely chopped
    pecans
2 tablespoons all-purpose flour
6 large eggs, separated
¾ cup plus 2 tablespoons sugar
Pinch of salt
4 Seckel Pears in Maple Syrup (page
    139), drained
1 cup heavy cream

In a food processor finely grind the toasted pecans with the flour and set aside.

In a large bowl beat the egg yolks until thick and pale. Gradually beat in ½ cup of the sugar, continue beating until the mixture forms a ribbon, and set aside. In another large bowl beat the egg whites with the salt until frothy. Gradually beat in ¼ cup of the sugar and continue beating until stiff peaks form.

Fold the toasted pecan mixture into the yolk mixture gently but thoroughly. Lighten the mixture with a generous spoonful of the meringue. Gradually fold the lightened nut mixture into the remaining meringue, being careful not to deflate the batter.

Pour the batter into a buttered and floured 9-inch springform pan and bake the torte in a preheated 350° oven for 45 to 50 minutes, or until it has pulled away from the sides of the pan. Let the torte cool in the pan on a rack for 30 minutes.

While the torte is cooling, halve the pears, remove the cores with a melon-ball scoop, and slice each half into 6 to 8 thin slices. Set aside. Beat the cream with the remaining 2 tablespoons sugar until soft peaks form.

Invert the torte onto a 10-inch removable tart pan base. Halve the torte horizontally, spread half the whipped cream on the bottom half, and arrange the pear slices on the cream. Replace the top half of the torte and spread the remaining whipped cream over the top and sides. Press the chopped pecans onto the sides. Chill the torte, covered loosely, for at least 1 hour or up to 6 hours before serving.

Serves 8 to 10

POACHED PEARS IN BLACK CURRANT VINEGAR SYRUP

The vinegar syrup adds a sharp edge to the taste of these pears, which makes them a wonderful addition to duck or other game ragouts.

2½ cups sugar
6 to 7 pounds firm-ripe pears, preferably Bartlett
6 allspice berries
3-inch cinnamon stick
4 whole cloves
Zest of 1 lemon
6 tablespoons black currant vinegar plus additional if necessary
6 bay leaves

In a large preserving pan combine the sugar and 6 cups water and cook over low heat, stirring occasionally, until the sugar is dissolved.

Peel the pears, 1 at a time, with a sharp knife, carefully halve them lengthwise, leaving one half of the stem on each half, and remove the cores with a melon-ball scoop, discarding any fibers. As you work, drop each pear half into the syrup to prevent discoloration.

Tie the allspice, cinnamon stick, and cloves loosely in a piece of cheesecloth and add the spices to the syrup. Add the lemon zest strips. Bring the syrup slowly to a boil over moderate heat and simmer the pears for 30 to 40 minutes, or until they are soft in the center when pierced with a skewer.

Divide the pears among three warm 1-quart jars and add 2 tablespoons vinegar and 2 bay leaves to each jar.

Remove the spice bag from the syrup, and reduce the syrup over high heat to about 5 cups, and strain it into a large pitcher. Divide the syrup among the jars, topping off each jar with extra vinegar to reach the desired level if necessary. Seal the jars and process them in a boiling water bath for 45 minutes. Let the jars cool completely before checking the seals and storing.

Makes 3 quarts

GREENGAGE PLUM JAM

The following method for making jam produces a concentrated fruit flavor; the fruit is cooked in its own juices after macerating in sugar. Other varieties of plums, such as Santa Rosas or Damsons, can be substituted.

6 pounds firm-ripe greengage plums
3 to 4 pounds (6 to 8 cups) sugar
2 tablespoons fresh lemon juice

Halve and pit the plums. Weigh the fruit and weigh out ½ to ¾ pound sugar (depending upon the sweetness of the fruit) per 1 pound fruit.

Layer the fruit and sugar in a large bowl and let it macerate, covered, for at least 8 hours or overnight.

Transfer the plum mixture to a preserving pan and bring the liquid to a boil over low heat. Add the lemon juice and simmer the mixture for 30 to 40 minutes, or until the jellying point is reached.

Spoon the jam into warm sterilized jars and seal.

Makes 1½ quarts

PRUNES IN YUNNAN TEA AND ARMAGNAC

Most plums can be dried, and one of the most flavorful and best-known varieties for drying is the plum from Agen, a town in southwestern France. In Agen the plums are sun-dried and remain soft and flavorful. Armagnac, a distilled wine, is another product of this region, making this a likely combination.

> ½ cup Yunnan tea leaves, or other smoky-flavored tea such as Lapsang Souchong
> 4 pounds soft unsulphured unpitted prunes
> 2 cups firmly packed light brown sugar
> 4 cups Armagnac
> 4 strips Dried Orange Peel (page 129)

In a saucepan bring 2 quarts water to a boil. In a large bowl pour the boiling water over the tea leaves and let the tea brew for 5 minutes.

Place the prunes in a large bowl. Strain the tea over the prunes and let the mixture cool. Cover the prunes and let them soak overnight.

In a saucepan combine the brown sugar with 2 cups water, bring the mixture to a boil, and simmer it, stirring, until the sugar is dissolved. Let the sugar syrup cool and add the Armagnac.

Drain the prunes and pat them dry. Divide the prunes among four 1-quart jars. Add a strip of orange peel to each jar, add the syrup and seal and jars. Process the jars in a cold water bath for 15 minutes. Let the jars cool completely before checking the seals and storing.

Makes 4 quarts

PLUM CHUTNEY

This chutney is a good accompaniment to cold meats and sharp Cheddar cheese and is also a good marinade for pork or chicken (see Chicken and Plum Chutney Kebabs on page 147).

> 2 pounds firm-ripe plums
> 2 pounds cooking apples
> 1 pound onions, thinly sliced
> 2 garlic cloves, minced
> 1-inch piece of fresh ginger, peeled and minced
> 1 tablespoon mustard seeds
> 1 tablespoon salt
> 2 cups red wine vinegar
> 2⅓ cups firmly packed light brown sugar

Quarter and pit the plums. Peel, core, and coarsely chop the apples.

In a preserving pan combine the plums, apples, onions, garlic, ginger, mustard seeds, and salt. Bring the mixture to a boil over low heat, and simmer it for 30 minutes, or until the ingredients are softened and can be easily crushed with the back of a spoon against the side of the pan.

Add the vinegar and brown sugar and cook the chutney for 30 to 45 minutes, or until it is thickened and the vinegar is absorbed.

Spoon the chutney into warm sterilized jars and seal. Store the unopened jars in a cool, dark place for at least 6 weeks before eating.

Makes 3 quarts

The French Agen prunes are traditionally paired with Armagnac. The prunes and alcohol can be enjoyed as an after-dinner digestive or swirled into vanilla ice cream.

CHICKEN AND PLUM CHUTNEY KEBABS

This plum chutney marinade can be used on pieces of chicken to be baked or grilled and is also good with pork. Serve the chicken with basmati rice, hot pappadums (crisp lentil wafers), and additional plum chutney.

2 pounds chicken thighs
1 cup Plum Chutney (page 144)
½ cup plain yogurt
½ teaspoon chili powder
½ teaspoon turmeric
2 tablespoons olive oil
¼ pound pearl onions, peeled
1 pound zucchini, cut into 1-inch
  rounds

Skin the chicken thighs and with a cleaver cut them into 1½-inch pieces, including the bone.

Pass the chutney through a sieve set over a large bowl, pressing hard with a spoon. Stir in the yogurt, chili powder, turmeric, and oil. Add the chicken to the yogurt mixture and let it marinate, covered, at room temperature for several hours.

Thread the chicken alternately with the onions and zucchini onto 4 skewers. Reserve the marinade. Cook the kebabs on a grill over hot coals or broil them, basting them with the marinade and turning them frequently, for 15 minutes.

Serves 4

147

DAMSON CONSERVES

Technically speaking, a conserve is a jam made by combining fruits, including citrus fruits, with raisins and nuts. Conserves are generally runny and are often referred to as spoon sweets, meaning, literally, to be eaten by the spoon.

    4 pounds damson plums
    1 orange, unpeeled, seeded, and cut
        into pieces
    1 lemon, unpeeled, seeded, and cut
        into pieces
    2 cups dried currants or chopped dates
    4 cups sugar
    2 cups coarsely chopped walnuts
    ½ teaspoon ground cardamom
    ½ teaspoon ground cinnamon

Quarter and pit the plums. Grind the orange and lemon in a meat grinder fitted with a coarse disk or in a food processor until coarsely chopped but not puréed.

In a large bowl combine the plums, orange, lemon, currants, and sugar and let the mixture stand, covered, overnight.

Transfer the mixture to a preserving pan, bring it to a boil over low heat, and boil it, stirring frequently, for about 45 minutes, or until the jellying point is reached. Stir in the chopped nuts and the spices.

Spoon the jam into warm sterilized jars and seal.

Makes 1½ quarts

DAMSON ICE CREAM

The ice cream can also be made with other fruit conserves, such as Cranberry, Pear, and Pecan Conserve (page 94).

    2 cups milk
    3-inch cinnamon stick
    6 large egg yolks
    ⅔ cup sugar
    1 cup Damson Conserves (above)

In a saucepan bring the milk to a boil with the cinnamon stick and let the mixture stand, covered, for 15 to 20 minutes.

In a bowl whisk the egg yolks until they are pale and fluffy. Gradually beat in the sugar. Remove the cinnamon stick from the milk and add the milk to the eggs in a thin stream, whisking.

Transfer the custard to the saucepan and cook it over low heat until it is thickened and coats the back of a wooden spoon. Strain the custard into a metal bowl over ice and let it cool, stirring occasionally.

Pour the custard into an ice-cream freezer and freeze it according to the manufacturer's instructions. When the ice cream is set, add the conserves and churn the mixture a few times to swirl the fruit into the ice cream. (Do not overblend.)

Makes 1 quart

P.D.'S QUINCE MARMALADE

Quince marmalade is a stock item at Pitts Deep, the country cottage of my friends the Campbells. This recipe produces a cross between a marmalade and a jelly.

    4 pounds quinces
    4 cups sugar
    ¼ cup fresh lemon juice

Coarsely chop half the quinces, including their peels and cores, and reserve the remaining 2 pounds. Combine the chopped fruit with 4 cups water in a preserving pan, bring the water to a boil over low heat, and simmer the fruit for 30 to 45 minutes, or until it is very soft.

Tip the contents of the pan into a dampened jelly bag set over a large bowl and let it drain at least 12 hours or overnight.

Combine the juice and sugar in the preserving pan and cook over low heat, stirring frequently, until the sugar is dissolved.

While the mixture is cooking slowly, peel and core the remaining 2 pounds quinces and either slice the fruit into thin shreds or chop it into coarse dice.

Bring the syrup to a boil, add the shredded or chopped fruit, and the lemon juice, and simmer the fruit, skimming any froth from the surface, for 30 minutes, or until it is softened. Bring the liquid back to a boil and continue cooking for about 15 minutes, or until the jelling point is reached.

Spoon the jam into warm sterilized jars and seal.

Makes 3 quarts

SLOE GIN

The sloe, or blackthorn, is a wild plum that grows on small trees or matted bushes usually found in neglected hedgerows. The little black berries, about ½ inch in diameter, have an astringent taste and therefore are not enjoyed as a fruit that is eaten out of hand. In England the berries are used to flavor gin: The sloes are gathered in October, and the resulting alcohol is first sipped at Christmas. The amount of sugar in traditional recipes can range from a few tablespoons up to 2 cups per pound of fruit. I find that the following proportions work well, providing a mild-flavored gin with a barely perceptible sweetness.

1 pound ripe sloes
3 tablespoons sugar
1 bottle (750 ml) gin
1 to 2 bitter almonds, if available

In a 1-quart jar combine the sloes with the sugar, gin, and almonds and let the mixture stand in a cool, dark place for at least 2 months or up to 6 months. Invert the jar and then right it once a week for the first few weeks to help distribute the sugar.

Strain the liquid through a sieve lined with a double layer of dampened cheesecloth into a bowl, discarding the solids. Funnel the gin into a bottle with a tight-fitting lid or cork. The gin will keep indefinitely.

Makes 1 quart

Award-winning homemade fruit wines at the summer Agricultural Show at Brightstone, Isle of Wight.

RASPBERRY HAZELNUT MERINGUE TORTE

The hazelnut meringue can be prepared up to two days in advance and the layers can be assembled with the cream and fruit several hours before serving.

    8 large egg whites
    Pinch of salt
    1 cup granulated sugar
    1 cup hazelnuts, toasted, skinned, and
        finely ground
    1½ cups heavy cream
    1½ cups drained Raspberries in Eau-
        de-Vie (page 151), plus
        2 tablespoons of the *eau-de-vie*
    Confectioners' sugar, for dusting

In a large bowl beat the egg whites with the salt until soft peaks form. Gradually add ¾ cup of the granulated sugar and continue beating until stiff peaks form. Fold in the hazelnuts. Divide the meringue between two 8-inch round buttered cake pans and bake in a preheated 275° oven for 20 minutes. Turn off the heat and let the meringues dry in the oven for 2 hours.

Carefully unmold the meringues and with a serrated knife halve each round horizontally, forming 4 meringue rounds.

Beat the heavy cream with the remaining ¼ cup granulated sugar and the *eau-de-vie* until soft peaks form.

On a serving dish spread 1 meringue round with one-third of the whipped cream and arrange ½ cup of the raspberries on the cream. Top the berries with another meringue round, half the remaining whipped cream, and ½ cup of the remaining berries. Add a third meringue round and the remaining cream and berries and finish with the fourth meringue round, cut-side down. Dust with the confectioners' sugar.

Serves 12

RASPBERRY VINEGAR

Raspberry vinegar is not an indispensable item for every kitchen, but for anyone blessed with excess raspberries that are too mature for preserving this is a worthwhile exercise. Raspberry vinegar is good sprinkled over fruit salads, in mayonnaise for cold meats, and as a deglazing agent for certain sauces based on meat juices.

    2 pints raspberries
    1 quart white wine vinegar

In a 2½- to 3-quart jar, preferably glass, with a nonreactive lid, combine the berries and the vinegar, seal the jar, and let the mixture stand for 3 weeks. (If possible, leave the jar in the sunlight, which will help draw out the fruit juices.)

Strain the vinegar into a large saucepan through a double layer of dampened cheesecloth and boil it over high heat until it is reduced by about one-fourth.

Ladle the vinegar into warm sterilized jars and seal.

Makes 1 quart

Layers of nut meringue and whipped cream are easily enhanced with a sprinkling of fruit preserved in alcohol such as the Raspberries in Eau-de-Vie used in Raspberry Hazelnut Meringue Torte.

GATEAU WEEKEND

This was one of the favorite recipes of Albert Jorant, pastry chef at the cooking school La Varenne, in Paris. The cake was given this name merely because it could be prepared mid-week and stored until the weekend. The original recipe, which is equally good if raspberries are not at hand, calls for jam or marmalade instead of the fruit in alcohol.

5 large eggs: 3 separated, 1 whole, plus
   1 extra egg white
1¼ cups sugar
1 cup ground almonds
½ cup unsweetened cocoa powder
⅓ cup all-purpose flour
½ teaspoon baking powder
Pinch of salt
3 tablespoons unsalted butter, melted
   and cooled
1 pound bittersweet chocolate
1⅓ cups heavy cream
1 cup drained raspberries from
   Raspberries in Eau-de-Vie (page
   151), plus ¼ cup *eau-de-vie* liquid

In a bowl with an electric mixer beat the 3 egg yolks and the 1 whole egg until they are thick and pale. Gradually beat in ½ cup of the sugar, beating until the mixture is very light and fluffy. Fold in the almonds.

Sift together the cocoa, flour, baking powder, and salt and fold the dry ingredients into the egg mixture alternately with the melted butter.

In another bowl beat the 4 egg whites until soft peaks form. Gradually beat in ¼ cup of the sugar, and continue beating until the meringue forms stiff peaks.

Lighten the chocolate mixture by beating about one-fourth of the meringue into it; and then gently fold in the remaining whites. Pour the batter into a buttered and floured 9 x 4 x 3-inch loaf pan and bake in a preheated 350° oven for 40 to 45 minutes, or until a skewer inserted in the center comes out clean. Let the cake cool in the pan on a rack.

While the cake is baking coarsely chop the bittersweet chocolate and transfer it to a heatproof bowl. In a saucepan heat the cream just to a boil, pour it over the chocolate, and stir the mixture until it is combined well. Chill the filling until it is firm, about 2 hours.

In a small saucepan combine the remaining ½ cup sugar with ½ cup water and heat the mixture gently over low heat, stirring, until the sugar is dissolved. Bring the syrup to a boil, boil it for 1 minute, and let it cool. Stir in the ¼ cup *eau-de-vie* liquid.

Slice the cake horizontally into 4 layers, and brush the bottom 3 layers with the *eau-de-vie* syrup. Spread ⅓ cup of the raspberries on each of the 3 moistened surfaces and set the layers aside.

Transfer half the chilled chocolate filling to a bowl (returning the remaining half to the refrigerator) and beat it until it is fluffy. Using about half of the whipped filling, spread it over the raspberries on the 3 layers and reassemble the layers to re-form the whole cake. Spread the remaining whipped filling over the top and sides of the cake, smoothing the surface. Chill the cake until it is firm, about 2 hours.

To finish the cake, in a heavy saucepan gently heat the reserved chocolate-cream mixture, stirring, until it is just melted. Put the cake on a rack over a sheet of wax paper and pour the warm chocolate over the cake to provide a smooth glossy finish. Let the glaze set at room temperature for a few hours before serving.

Makes 1 loaf cake

ROWANBERRY AND CRABAPPLE JELLY

Rowanberries are the fruit of the common mountain ash. The berries are dark orange and inedible in their raw state—except by cedar waxwings who enjoy feasting off the trees. The tart jelly from this fruit is best used as an accompaniment to meat, much as mint jelly is so often used. A tablespoon or so can also be added to deglaze juices in a skillet or used as a base for a sauce.

1½ pounds rowanberries
1½ pounds crabapples
3 cups sugar

Coarsely chop the rowanberries and crabapples. In a preserving pan combine the fruit with 3 cups water. Bring the water to a boil over low heat and simmer the fruit for 45 minutes to 1 hour, or until it is very soft and can be crushed against the side of the pan with the back of a spoon.

Tip the contents of the pan into a dampened jelly bag set over a large bowl and let it drain for at least 12 hours or overnight.

Measure 4 cups of the juice and transfer it back to the preserving pan. Add the sugar and heat the mixture over low heat, stirring, until the sugar is dissolved. Bring the sugar syrup to a boil and cook it, skimming frequently, for 25 minutes, or until the jellying point is reached.

Ladle the jelly into small warm sterilized jars and seal.

Makes 3 cups

POPOVERS WITH ROWANBERRY AND CRABAPPLE JELLY

Popovers are quick to make and are a good accompaniment, when filled with a tart jelly, to roasted game birds or sautéed duck breasts.

2 large eggs
1 cup milk
1 tablespoon unsalted butter, melted and cooled
1 cup all-purpose flour
½ teaspoon salt
½ cup Rowanberry and Crabapple Jelly (at left)

Brush eight ½-cup custard cups or cast-iron muffin tins with vegetable oil and preheat them in a 450° oven for 10 minutes. Leave the oven on.

While the custard cups are heating, in a bowl whisk together the eggs, milk, and butter. Sift the flour and salt, a little at a time, over the milk mixture and whisk just to combine.

Fill the hot custard cups one-third full and bake the popovers for 15 minutes. Reduce the heat to 350° and bake them for 15 minutes more, or until they are nicely browned.

Pierce the center of each popover with the tip of a sharp knife and add a tablespoon of the jelly to each one. Serve the popovers immediately.

Makes 8

STRAWBERRY JAM BEIGNETS

Homemade doughnuts are best eaten within a couple of hours of cooking. If you like, substitute other fruit jams or jellies for the strawberry jam.

3 tablespoons active dry yeast (three to four ¼-ounce packages)
1 cup lukewarm milk
⅓ cup plus 1 tablespoon granulated sugar
2 large eggs
½ cup unsalted butter, melted

Pinch of salt
About 4 cups all-purpose flour
1 cup Strawberry Jewels (page 158)
Vegetable oil, for deep-frying
Superfine or confectioners' sugar, for dusting

In a small bowl proof the yeast in the milk with 1 tablespoon of the granulated sugar for 5 minutes, or until it is foamy.

In a large bowl beat the eggs with the remaining ⅓ cup granulated sugar until the eggs are pale and lemon-colored. Add the butter and the yeast mixture and combine

the mixture well. Stir in the salt and enough of the flour to form a soft dough. Knead the dough on a floured surface for 5 to 8 minutes, or until it is smooth and elastic.

Transfer the dough to a lightly buttered bowl, turn it to coat it with the butter, and let the dough rise, covered, in a warm place for 1 hour, or until it is doubled in bulk.

Punch down the dough and roll it out ¼ inch thick on a floured surface. Using a 3-inch cutter dipped in flour, cut 32 rounds, rerolling and cutting the scraps.

Put 1 tablespoon of the jam in the center of half the rounds and cover with the re-maining rounds, pressing the edges to seal them. Place the beignets on a floured baking sheet. Let them rise, covered, in a warm place for 30 minutes, or until they are doubled in bulk.

In a deep-fryer heat 3 inches vegetable oil to 360° and deep-fry the beignets in batches for 1 to 2 minutes on each side, or until they are golden and puffed. Transfer the beignets with a slotted spoon to paper towels to drain. Sprinkle the beignets with superfine or confectioners' sugar.

Makes 16

157

STRAWBERRY JEWELS

This is a French technique for making strawberry jam. The berries are repeatedly plunged into a boiling sugar syrup to rapidly remove their excess moisture and to cut down on cooking time. The syrup is reduced to concentrate the berry flavor, and the whole strawberries are re-introduced to the transparent jelly—possessing a gemlike clarity.

5 pounds strawberries, hulled
5 cups sugar
¼ cup fresh lemon juice

In a large shallow bowl sprinkle half the strawberries with 1 cup of the sugar. Add the remaining strawberries and sprinkle them with another 1 cup sugar. Cover and let the strawberries stand at room temperature overnight.

Transfer the berry mixture to a colander set over a preserving pan and let the juices drain into the pan, reserving the berries. Stir the remaining 3 cups sugar into the pan and cook the juice mixture over low heat, stirring, until the sugar is dissolved.

Bring the syrup to a boil and add the reserved strawberries and lemon juice. Boil the mixture for 5 minutes. With a slotted spoon transfer the berries to the colander, set over a bowl.

Boil the syrup for 5 minutes, or until it is reduced slightly. Add any strawberry juices that have accumulated in the bowl and continue boiling to reduce the mixture by the amount added.

Add the berries to the syrup once again and boil for about 5 minutes, or until the jellying point is reached. Remove the pan from the heat and allow the jam to stand for 10 minutes.

Spoon the jam into warm sterilized jars and seal.

Makes 1½ quarts

MIXED DRIED FRUITS IN MARSALA

Home-dried rather than commercially dried fruits are best in this preparation; among the latter, however, be sure to choose unsweetened and preferably untreated types. Substitute other fruits for those listed below according to personal preference.

About 1½ cups sugar
Zest of 1 orange
Zest of 1 lemon
1 pound dried whole apricots
½ pound Dried Apple Rings (page 65)
½ pound Dried Cherries (page 83) or
  Dried Cranberries (page 93)
½ pound dried pear halves
½ pound pitted prunes
2 cups Marsala

In a large saucepan combine the sugar with 6 cups water and the zests and cook the mixture over low heat, stirring occasionally, until the sugar is dissolved. Bring the liquid to a boil, add the dried fruits, and simmer them for 20 minutes. Let the fruit cool completely in the syrup.

Divide the fruit with a slotted spoon among four warm 1½-pint jars and add ½ cup of the Marsala to each.

Bring the syrup in the pan to a boil, strain it into the jars, and seal. Process the jars in a boiling water bath for 20 minutes. Let the jars cool completely before checking the seals and storing.

Makes 3 quarts

CRANBERRY, SHALLOT, AND CURRANT RELISH

This relish is delicious with cold meat, particularly leftover roast turkey or pork.

1 cup thinly sliced shallots
3 tablespoons vegetable oil
1½ cups sugar
3 tablespoons grated orange zest
1 tablespoon minced fresh ginger
1 cup dried currants
1½ cups fresh orange juice
½ cup red wine vinegar
4 cups cranberries

In a large nonreactive saucepan cook the shallots in the oil over low heat for 5 minutes, or until softened. Stir in the sugar, zest, ginger, currants, orange juice, and vinegar and cook the mixture over low heat, stirring, until the sugar is dissolved.

Bring the mixture to a boil, stir in the cranberries, and boil the mixture, stirring occasionally, for 30 minutes, or until it is thickened and all the liquid is absorbed.

Spoon the relish into warm 1-pint jars and seal. Process the jars in a boiling water bath for 10 minutes. Let cool completely before checking the seals and storing.

Makes 1½ quarts

MODERN MINCEMEAT

Traditional mincemeat is made from "minced" or ground beef, suet, dried fruit, sugar, spices, and an abundant amount of brandy or Sherry. The alcohol and sugar not only enhance flavor but also help to preserve the meat. Mincemeat is used most frequently during the Christmas holidays for pie and tartlet fillings. The following recipe is a meatless version but does include suet, which provides a rich, moist filling for any subsequent use.

1 pound cooking apples
1 pound pears
½ pound dried apricots
½ pound Dried Cherries (page 83)
½ pound dried dates
½ pound dried figs
½ pound dark raisins
½ pound Malaga or Muscat raisins
1 pound beef suet, minced or grated
1 pound light brown sugar
Grated zest and juice of 2 lemons
½ cup Apricot Jam (page 68)
1 teaspoon ground allspice
1 teaspoon ground cinnamon
½ teaspoon freshly grated nutmeg
½ teaspoon ground cloves
½ teaspoon ground ginger
¾ cup brandy
¾ cup Sherry

Peel, core, and coarsely chop the apples and pears and combine them in a large bowl. Coarsely chop the apricots, cherries, dates, and figs and add them to the bowl.

Stir in all the remaining ingredients and let macerate, stirring the mixture every other day and adding more alcohol if necessary to keep it moist, for 1 week.

Pack the mincemeat into sterilized jars and seal. Store the unopened jars in a cool, dark place for at least 1 month before using.

Makes 4 quarts

MINCEMEAT CHRISTMAS STARS WITH ORANGE SAUCE

1 cup firmly packed light brown sugar
½ cup clear honey
1½ sticks (¾ cup) unsalted butter
4 cups all-purpose flour
1 tablespoon baking soda
1 tablespoon ground ginger
Pinch of salt
2 large eggs, well beaten
1 tablespoon grated orange zest
¾ cup fresh orange juice
2 tablespoons brandy
About 3 cups Modern Mincemeat
   (page 159)
Confectioners' sugar, for dusting

In a saucepan heat ½ cup of the brown sugar, the honey, and 6 tablespoons of the butter over low heat, stirring, until the butter is melted and the sugar dissolved. Let cool slightly.

Sift the flour, baking soda, ginger, and salt together in a large bowl and make a well in the center. Stir the eggs into the cooled butter mixture and pour the mixture into the well. Gradually draw the flour into the center and continue to stir until all the flour is incorporated and the dough forms a ball. Wrap the dough in wax paper and chill it for 30 minutes.

Roll the dough ¼ inch thick and cut out star shapes with a 3½-inch cutter or template. Reroll and cut the scraps in the same manner. (There should be about 16.) On a buttered baking sheet bake the stars in a preheated 350° oven for 8 minutes, or until they are golden, and transfer them to wire racks to cool.

In a saucepan, combine the remaining ½ cup brown sugar and 6 tablespoons butter with the zest and orange juice and stir over low heat until the sugar is dissolved. Remove the mixture from the heat, stir in the brandy, and keep the sauce warm.

Remove the flaky top layer from each star by running a knife just inside the edges of the stars and lifting off the loosened pastry. (This should provide a case for the mincemeat.) Spoon 2 to 3 tablespoons of the mincemeat into the center of each star.

Smooth about 2 tablespoons orange sauce in each of 8 dessert plates, top with 2 stars, and sprinkle with confectioners' sugar.

Serves 8

A Christmas tea in London by the fireplace. The selection includes Mincemeat Christmas Stars with Orange Sauce, Kumquats in Brandy, and jam and fruit curd tartlets.

SEMOLINA SAVARINS WITH THREE MERRY BERRIES

5 large eggs, separated
½ cup sugar
Grated zest and juice of 1 lemon
¾ cup finely ground semolina
½ cup finely ground almonds
1 cup drained mixed berries from
  Three Merry Berries in Raspberry
  Eau-de-Vie (at right), plus 1 cup of
  the *eau-de-vie*
1 cup heavy cream
Mint sprigs, for garnish

In a bowl beat the egg yolks with ¼ cup of the sugar until the mixture is thick and pale and ribbons when the whisk (or beater) is lifted. Beat in the zest.

In a large bowl beat the egg whites until they form soft peaks. Add the remaining ¼ cup sugar and continue beating until they form stiff glossy peaks.

Combine the semolina, almonds, and lemon juice in a bowl and in 3 batches fold the dry mixture and the whites alternately into the yolk mixture gently but thoroughly.

Divide the batter among 8 buttered 3-inch savarin molds (or turn it into 1 buttered 9-inch savarin mold) and bake in a preheated 350° oven for 12 to 15 minutes (25 to 30 minutes for the 9-inch mold), or until the savarins pull away slightly from the sides of the molds and the tops are springy to the touch. Turn the savarins out of the molds onto a rack and let them cool.

Heat the *eau-de-vie* until it is warm to the touch. Put the rack of savarins over a rimmed baking sheet and spoon the *eau-de-vie* over them, letting the liquid accumulate on the baking sheet and basting the savarins until all the liquid is absorbed.

In a bowl beat the cream until soft peaks form. Transfer the savarins to serving plates and garnish them with the berries, the whipped cream, and the mint.

Serves 8

THREE MERRY BERRIES IN RASPBERRY EAU-DE-VIE

This recipe is a variation of the classic American rum pot. The principle is to preserve a combination of fruits in a large crock with sugar and spirits. The various fruits are added in stages that are determined by when each variety reaches its seasonal peak. Once the crock is full, the fruits are generally left to macerate for at least one month before being eaten. The three berries in the following recipe are available at the same time during the summer and are therefore preserved simultaneously.

8 black currant leaves
½ pound strawberries, hulled
1 cup sugar
¾ pound black currants, stemmed
¾ pound raspberries
2½ cups raspberry *eau-de-vie*
  (framboise)

Line each of four 1-pint jars with 2 black currant leaves.

Divide the strawberries among the jars and sprinkle 2 tablespoons sugar into each jar.

Divide the black currants among the jars and sprinkle each layer with 2 tablespoons of the remaining sugar.

Divide the raspberries among the jars, pour enough of the *eau-de-vie* into each jar to cover the fruit, and seal. Store the unopened jars for at least 1 month before using.

Makes 2 quarts

*Individual savarins
made with semolina are
served with strawberries,
black currants, and
raspberries preserved in
raspberry eau-de-vie.*

VEGETABLES

MARINATED ARTICHOKES
IN OLIVE OIL

The small purple-tinged artichokes that appear in the spring are perfect for preserving in olive oil. After about 1 month, the preserved artichokes can be eaten as part of an antipasto, sautéed and served with pasta or rice, or in Marinated Artichoke, Ham, and Spinach Torte (page 170).

> 6 pounds small artichokes
> ¼ cup fresh lemon juice
> 6 cups white wine vinegar
> 3 cups dry white wine
> 1 tablespoon salt
> 1 teaspoon coriander seed
> 1 bay leaf
> 2 to 4 sprigs of fresh rosemary
> 4 cups extra-virgin olive oil

Trim the artichoke stems, remove any dried leaves, and trim the tips of each leaf with a pair of scissors. Halve the artichokes vertically and reserve them in a large bowl of water acidulated with the lemon juice.

In a large nonreactive saucepan combine the vinegar, wine, salt, coriander seed, and bay leaf and bring the liquid to a boil over low heat.

Drain the artichokes and add them to the boiling liquid. Bring the liquid back to a boil, reduce the heat, and simmer the artichokes for 10 minutes, or until they are tender. Transfer the artichokes to paper towels to drain.

Divide the artichokes between two sterilized 1½-quart jars and add a rosemary sprig or two to each one. Cover the artichokes completely with the oil and seal the jars. Store the unopened jars in a cool, dark place for at least 1 month before eating.

Makes 3 quarts

Above: a trained bay tree at The Royal Horticultural Garden, Wisley. Overleaf: rows of artichokes at their peak at Stowell Park, Gloucestershire.

MARINATED ARTICHOKE, HAM, AND SPINACH TORTE

This torte incorporates marinated artichokes with fresh spinach, tomatoes, and cheese. If you like, sun-dried tomatoes can be substituted for the fresh ones.

2 cups all-purpose flour
1 teaspoon salt
1 stick (½ cup) unsalted butter, cut into bits
Grated zest of 1 lemon
2 large egg yolks plus 1 large whole egg
12 Marinated Artichokes (page 167), drained, reserving 3 tablespoons oil
½ pound fresh spinach leaves
Freshly ground pepper
2 tomatoes, peeled, seeded, and coarsely chopped
1 teaspoon crumbled dried sage
¼ pound ham, cut into small cubes
½ pound Fontina, cut into small cubes

In a large bowl sift together the flour and salt and rub in the butter and zest until the mixture resembles coarse meal. In a small bowl beat the two egg yolks with ¼ cup ice-cold water and stir into the flour mixture, forming a ball. Wrap the dough in plastic wrap and chill it for 30 minutes.

While the dough is chilling, in a sauté pan heat 2 tablespoons of the reserved oil and in it sauté the spinach over high heat, stirring, for 1 minute, or until it is wilted. Season the spinach with salt and pepper to taste and transfer it to a plate.

Add the remaining 1 tablespoon reserved oil to the sauté pan and in it sauté the tomatoes, stirring, until all the moisture is evaporated. Season the tomatoes with the sage and salt and pepper to taste.

Halve the dough and on a lightly floured surface roll one half out to fit a 9-inch round tart pan with a removable rim, leaving a ¼-inch overhang. Prick the crust all over.

Spread half the spinach on the crust, and arrange the artichokes on top. Layer the tomatoes, ham, Fontina, and remaining spinach over the artichokes. Roll out the remaining dough, lay it over the filling, and crimp the edges of the top and bottom crusts decoratively.

Prick the top crust in several places with a fork. Beat the whole egg well and brush it over the top crust. Bake the torte in a preheated 425° oven for 12 minutes. Reduce the heat to 325° and continue baking for 30 minutes, or until the pastry is golden. Let the torte cool for 15 to 20 minutes before slicing and serving. The torte can also be served at room temperature.

Serves 6

PICKLED BABY BEETS

Small beets are the most attractive to preserve. The same method can be used, however, for larger beets. You need only cook them until they are tender, then peel them, slice them into thick rounds, and proceed as with the small beets.

3 pounds baby beets, trimmed
3 cups cider vinegar
2 teaspoons salt
2 tablespoons honey
About 6 allspice berries

In a large saucepan of boiling salted water cook the beets for 15 minutes, or until tender. Drain the beets and let them cool.

In a nonreactive saucepan bring the vinegar, salt, and honey to a boil; let cool.

When the beets are cool enough to handle, peel them and divide them among sterilized jars. Add 2 allspice berries to each jar, cover the beets with the vinegar mixture, and seal the jars. Store the unopened jars in a cool, dark place for at least 1 week before eating.

Makes 3 pints

CARROT JAM

This jam is delicious spread on toasted brioche or quick bread nut loaves. It is also good when used to flavor plain yogurt.

1 lemon, unpeeled, seeded, and
  coarsely chopped
1 orange, unpeeled, seeded, and
  coarsely chopped
2 pounds carrots, shredded
2 cups sugar
½ cup Apple Pectin Stock
  (page 63)
1 teaspoon ground cardamom

Finely grind the lemon and orange in a food processor. Steam the shredded carrots for 5 minutes and let them cool.

In a preserving pan combine the sugar with the lemon and orange and apple pectin stock. Cook over low heat until the sugar is dissolved, then bring to a boil.

Add the carrots to the syrup and boil them, stirring frequently, for about 30 minutes, or until the jelling point is reached. Stir in the cardamom.

Spoon the jam into warm sterilized jars and seal.

Makes 1 quart

PICKLED RED CABBAGE

Red cabbage can be preserved as a pickle, although its storage life is limited to 3 to 4 weeks if perfect results are to be maintained. If stored longer, the cabbage tends to lose its crunch.

  4 large heads of red cabbage
  ½ cup coarse sea salt
  ¼ cup firmly packed light brown sugar
  1 medium red onion, sliced into thin rings
  About 12 juniper berries
  4 bay leaves
  About 4 cups red wine vinegar

Quarter and core the cabbages and cut them into very thin shreds. Layer the cabbage on a large nonreactive tray (preferably stainless steel or plastic) and sprinkle with the salt and brown sugar. Toss the mixture and let it stand for 2 hours.

Squeeze the excess moisture from the cabbage, a handful at a time, and pack the cabbage and onion in alternating layers into four sterilized 1-pint jars. Tuck a few juniper berries into each jar and slide 1 bay leaf down the side of each jar between the cabbage and the glass.

Add about 1 cup vinegar to each jar and seal. Store the unopened jars in a cool, dark place for at least 4 days before eating.

Makes 2 quarts

The kitchen garden at Hunstrete House Hotel, Avon, supplies summer produce for guests.

SAUERKRAUT

Sauerkraut is simply fermented cabbage. The transformation occurs by adding salt to shredded cabbage, which ferments over a period of two to three weeks as the vegetable sugars are converted into acids by microorganisms within the cabbage. The fermentation produces a froth, and once the froth has subsided, the cabbage has become sauerkraut.

15 to 16 pounds firm white cabbage
  (about 5 heads)
6 ounces (about ¾ cup) coarse sea salt
¼ cup caraway seeds
2 tablespoons juniper berries

Remove the tough outer leaves from the cabbage and discard them. Line the base of a 2- to 2½-gallon glazed stoneware crock with some of the tender leaves.

Halve the cabbages, remove the cores, and slice the halves into thin shreds. Weigh the sliced cabbage and measure out 2 ounces (¼ cup) sea salt for every 5 pounds cabbage. Toss the cabbage and salt together in a very large bowl (or bowls) and let stand for 15 minutes, or until the cabbage has softened.

Layer the cabbage mixture into the crock, sprinkling each layer with some of the caraway seeds and juniper berries. (Make sure that each layer of cabbage is firmly packed down before adding the next layer.) Add any juices from the bowl(s).

Cover the cabbage with a double layer of clean cheesecloth and a dinner plate that is just large enough to fit inside the crock. Fill a 2-quart jar with water, seal it, and set it on top of the plate to weight the cabbage layers.

Leave the crock at room temperature (68° to 72° F.) for about 1 week, or until froth appears around the edges. Remove the jar of water, plate, and cheesecloth and skim off the froth.

Repeat the weighting and skimming process, using a clean piece of cheesecloth and letting the mixture ferment for another day or two. Repeat the process every few days for about 2 more weeks, or until all the frothing ceases. The sauerkraut is ready to eat at this stage. It may be kept, chilled, for 1 month. For longer storage, the sauerkraut may be frozen in handy-to-use packs, or it may be brought just to the boiling point over low heat, ladled into warm jars, and processed in a boiling water bath: 15 minutes for jars up to 1 pint, 20 minutes for jars up to 1 quart.

Makes 1½ to 2 gallons

TANGY CAULIFLOWERS

Pickled cauliflower makes a humble addition to an antipasto platter or can be enjoyed on its own, garnished with a few red onion slices and parsley.

3 pounds cauliflower, separated into
  flowerets
3 cups white wine vinegar
½ cup coarse sea salt
4 Dried Hot Chilies (page 225)
1 tablespoon allspice berries

Blanch the cauliflower in a large saucepan of boiling salted water for 5 minutes, drain it, and let it cool.

In a large nonreactive saucepan combine the vinegar with the salt and 1 cup water. Bring to a boil and boil for 5 minutes.

Pack the cauliflower attractively in four warm sterilized 1-pint jars, adding 1 chili and some of the allspice berries to each jar.

Pour in enough of the vinegar mixture to cover the cauliflower and seal the jars. Store the unopened jars in a cool, dark place for at least 2 weeks before eating.

Makes 2 quarts

CHICKEN STEW WITH DRIED CORN AND CORIANDER

This stew can be prepared a couple of days in advance and reheated in a moderate oven before serving. Other vegetables such as zucchini, green beans, and potatoes can be included for variation.

1 cup Jane's Dried Corn (page 176)
2 whole chicken breasts, skinned and halved
1 tablespoon ground cumin
3 cups chicken stock
1 pound carrots, quartered lengthwise and cut into 2-inch pieces
½ pound snow peas
1 cup heavy cream
Salt and freshly ground pepper
¼ cup fresh coriander leaves

In a small bowl combine the dried corn with 2 cups boiling-hot water and let it soften for 1 hour.

In a shallow casserole poach the chicken breasts with the cumin in the stock for 20 minutes. Transfer the chicken to a plate with tongs. Boil the stock over moderately high heat until it is reduced to about 2 cups.

While the broth is reducing, in a saucepan cook the carrots in boiling salted water for 10 to 12 minutes, or until they are tender. Transfer the carrots to a bowl with a slotted spoon and in the boiling water blanch the snow peas for 2 to 3 minutes. Drain the snow peas, refresh them under cold running water, and add them to the bowl with the carrots.

When the chicken is cool enough to handle, remove the meat from the bones in large sections and slice each breast diagonally into 4 or 5 slices.

Drain the corn and add it, the cream, and salt and pepper to taste to the reduced broth. Bring the liquid to a boil and simmer it for 20 to 30 minutes, or until the corn is tender and the sauce is reduced by ½ cup.

Add the chicken, carrots, and snow peas to the sauce, simmer the stew for about 10 minutes, or just long enough to heat it through. Ladle the stew into rimmed soup bowls and garnish it with the coriander leaves.

Serves 4 to 6

DRIED CORN CUSTARD

This custard can be served as a side dish with meat or poultry or, for a light meal, as a main course with a green salad.

1 cup Jane's Dried Corn (page 176)
2 cups milk, scalded
4 large eggs, well beaten
½ cup grated Cheddar
¼ teaspoon freshly grated nutmeg
1 teaspoon salt

In a bowl combine the corn and scalded milk and let the corn soften for 1 hour.

In a bowl whisk together the eggs, cheese, nutmeg, and salt. Add the mixture to the corn, whisking until the batter is well combined.

Transfer the batter to a buttered 1-quart shallow baking dish and bake the custard in a preheated 375° oven for 20 to 25 minutes, or until it is puffed and golden. Serve the custard either hot or at room temperature.

Serves 4

PICKLED GHERKINS

Gherkins, a special variety of cucumber, are picked and pickled when they are 1½ to 2 inches long. Pickled gherkins, or French *cornichons*, are essential accompaniments to pâtés, *rillettes*, and dried sausages.

    3 pounds fresh gherkins
    1 cup coarse sea salt
    6 cups white wine vinegar
    ¼ pound pearl onions, blanched and
        peeled
    6 bay leaves
    6 sprigs of fresh tarragon, blanched and
        patted dry
    6 Dried Hot Chilies (page 225)
    1 tablespoon allspice berries
    1 tablespoon black peppercorns
    1 tablespoon white peppercorns

Wash and scrub the gherkins to remove the spiny hairs, rub them dry, and mix them with the salt in a large bowl. Let the mixture stand, covered, overnight. (The salt will draw out the moisture.)

Drain the gherkins and in a large bowl immerse them in 2 cups of the vinegar and 2 cups water. Drain the gherkins immediately and pat them dry.

Divide the gherkins among six sterilized 1-pint jars, layering each jar with a few pearl onions, 1 bay leaf, 1 tarragon sprig, 1 hot chili, a few allspice berries, and some of the peppercorns.

Cover the gherkins with the remaining 4 cups vinegar and seal the jars. Store the unopened jars in a cool, dark place for at least 6 weeks before eating.

Makes 3 quarts

A ploughman's lunch at a traditional English pub: country ham, Cheddar cheese, and pickled onions, gherkins, and beets.

PICKLED PINK ONIONS

Select firm young white pearl onions—red pearl onions are equally good—for best results.

    4 pounds pearl onions
    ¾ cup coarse sea salt
    2 quarts red wine vinegar
    ½ cup fresh mint leaves, blanched and
        patted dry

In a large saucepan of boiling water blanch the pearl onions for about 1 minute. When they are cool enough to handle, peel them.

In a large bowl toss the onions and salt together and let stand for 3 hours. Rinse the salt off the onions by quickly immersing them in a large basin of cold water. Drain them and pat them dry thoroughly.

In a nonreactive saucepan boil the vinegar until reduced by half; let it cool.

Divide the onions and mint leaves among sterilized jars, add enough vinegar to cover the onions, and seal the jars. Store the unopened jars in a cool, dark place for at least 6 weeks before eating.

Makes 2 quarts

WILD MUSHROOM POWDER

Once wild mushrooms have been dried (see Dried Forest Mushrooms on page 181), they can be reduced to a powder to provide a convenient form of flavoring for savory sauces as well as soups and stews.

Simply crush a handful of dried mushrooms in a mortar with a pestle or pulverize them in a food processor. The powder may be limited to just one variety of mushroom, or can combine several types if you have them on hand.

Store the powder in airtight containers away from light for up to 1 year.

Preserved wild mushrooms in oil are combined with ham, sun-dried tomatoes, and parsley, and served with rounds of grilled polenta.

GRILLED POLENTA WITH MUSHROOM AND HAM RAGOUT

2 teaspoons salt
2 cups coarse yellow cornmeal
½ stick (¼ cup) unsalted butter
2 cups drained Wild Mushrooms in Oil (at right), plus ¼ cup of the oil
½ pound boiled ham, sliced into long strips
Freshly ground pepper
¼ cup minced flat-leaf parsley
About ¼ cup olive oil, for brushing the polenta
1 cup drained Sun-Dried Tomatoes (page 194), sliced into strips, for garnish

In a saucepan bring 6 cups water to a boil with the salt and add the cornmeal in a slow stream, whisking constantly. Simmer the mixture, stirring constantly, for 35 minutes, or until the cornmeal has absorbed all the moisture and forms a solid mass. Add 2 tablespoons of the butter to the polenta. Butter a baking sheet with the remaining 2 tablespoons butter and spread the polenta out to form a slab just under ½ inch thick. Let the polenta cool, about 45 minutes.

While the polenta is setting, in a saucepan heat the reserved ¼ cup mushroom oil over low heat. Add the mushrooms and ham and cook them until they are just heated through. Season with pepper to taste and add the parsley.

Cut the polenta into eight 2-inch rounds with a cutter and brush one side of each round with some of the olive oil. Grill the rounds, oiled-sides down, over hot coals for 3 to 4 minutes. Brush the tops with the remaining oil, turn the rounds, and cook them for 2 minutes more.

Put 2 rounds of polenta on each of 4 dinner plates, top them generously with the ham and mushroom mixture, and garnish with the sun-dried tomato slices.

Serves 4

WILD MUSHROOMS IN OIL

Mushrooms preserved in olive oil make a good first course, especially if they are sprinkled with fresh herbs and topped with a tomato *coulis*.

> 3 pounds fresh wild mushrooms, such as cèpes, parasols, or chanterelles
> 4 cups white wine vinegar
> 2 cups dry white wine
> ¼ cup coarse sea salt
> 3 tablespoons coriander seeds
> 4 bay leaves
> 1 sprig of fresh rosemary
> About 2 cups extra-virgin olive oil

Trim the stems of the mushrooms and wipe the caps clean with a dampened cloth.

In a large saucepan combine the vinegar and white wine with the salt, coriander seeds, 1 of the bay leaves, and the rosemary, bring the liquid to a boil over low heat, and simmer the mixture for 10 minutes.

Add half the mushrooms to the hot liquid and simmer them for 10 minutes. Transfer the mushrooms to a colander with a slotted spoon. Add the remaining mushrooms to the saucepan and simmer them for 10 minutes, then add them to the colander.

Pat the mushrooms dry with paper towels and divide them among three sterilized 1-pint jars. Tuck 1 bay leaf into each jar and add enough oil to each jar to cover the mushrooms. Seal the jars and store them, unopened, in a cool, dark place for at least 1 week before eating. Once the jars are opened, be sure the mushrooms remain immersed in oil to prevent them from spoiling.

Makes 3 pints

DRIED FOREST MUSHROOMS

Many varieties of wild mushroom can be preserved by dehydration, a simple technique that intensifies the flavor of the mushrooms. Dried mushrooms may be reconstituted in a little water or wine and used in egg, rice, and pasta dishes and in meat and poultry stuffings. For most soups, stews, and sauces they can be added directly to the liquid without being soaked.

Of all the wild mushrooms, field mushrooms (*Agaricus campestris*) are the most readily available in late summer fields. Other varieties, which are more cherished, include cèpes (*Boletus edulis*), fairy rings (*Marasmius oreades*), chanterelles (*Cantharellus cibarius*), horn of plenty (*Craterellus cornucopioides*), and morels (*Morchella esculenta*).

Important note: Not all wild mushrooms are edible and even many edible varieties have poisonous lookalikes. To avoid danger, wild mushrooms should be identified by an expert before consumption.

To prepare mushrooms for drying, trim the stem ends of all varieties and clean the caps by either wiping them with a dampened cloth or, in the case of morels, quickly submerging them in a basin of cold water two or three times.

Small mushrooms, such as fairy rings and chanterelles, can be dried whole; larger mushrooms, such as cèpes, should be sliced ¼ inch thick.

Spread the mushrooms out on a wire rack and dry them in a preheated 110° oven for 8 to 10 hours, or until completely dry to the touch. (Leave the door ajar to allow for good ventilation). Let the mushrooms cool completely before storing them in an airtight container. Alternatively the mushrooms may be dried by threading them on strings (making sure the mushrooms don't touch) and leaving them to dry in a low-humidity room for a few days.

PRESERVED EGGPLANT
IN OLIVE OIL

Preserved eggplant slices can be served as a first course with a pesto sauce or can be used as an ingredient for a vegetable gratin or as a topping for pizza, such as Cornmeal Pizza with Preserved Eggplants and Tomato Sauce (page 203).

5 to 6 pounds medium eggplants
⅓ cup coarse sea salt
6 cups white wine vinegar
About 4 cups extra-virgin olive oil
4 teaspoons coriander seeds
8 Dried Hot Chilies (page 225)

Slice the eggplants into ½-inch rounds and toss the rounds in a large bowl with the salt. On a large work surface covered with paper towels spread the slices out in a single layer, cover them with more paper towels, and weigh them down with a large cutting board or heavy baking sheets. Let the eggplant sweat for at least 1 hour.

In a large nonreactive saucepan bring the vinegar to a boil. Add the eggplant slices, bring the vinegar back to a boil, and simmer the eggplant for 5 minutes. Drain the eggplant and pat it dry.

Pour ½ inch of the oil in each of four sterilized 1-pint jars and divide the eggplant rounds among the jars. Add 1 teaspoon coriander seeds and 2 of the chilies, diced, to each jar. (Wear rubber gloves when cutting the chilies.) Add enough of the remaining oil to each jar to fill them.

Seal the jars and store them, unopened, in a cool, dark place for at least 1 week before eating. Once the jars are opened, be sure that the eggplant rounds remain immersed in oil to prevent them from spoiling.

Makes 2 quarts

*Slices of preserved eggplant and peppers
are seasoned with pesto sauce
and chili-flavored vinegar.*

GREEN OLIVES IN BRINE

Immature, green olives are very bitter when freshly picked and need to be treated to remove the excessive bitter flavor before preserving in brine. Commercial preparations often involve soaking whole olives in a lye solution or a solution of water and wood ash paste. If the green olives are a bit more mature (they will be darker in color), they can be cracked open and soaked in plain water, as in the recipe below. Choose olives that are as dark green as possible.

2 pounds dark green olives
1 cup coarse sea salt
1 strip of orange zest
1 head of garlic, whole and unpeeled
5 bay leaves
1 tablespoon coriander seeds

Crack each olive open by tapping with a mallet and combine the olives with enough cold water to cover in a large basin or crock. Let the olives soak for 10 days, changing the water every day.

In a large saucepan dissolve the salt in 2 quarts water over low heat, add the orange zest, garlic, and 1 bay leaf, and simmer the mixture for 15 minutes. Let the brine cool.

Drain the olives and divide them among four sterilized 1-pint jars. Add 1 bay leaf and a few coriander seeds to each jar. Strain the brine and add enough to each jar to cover the olives. Seal the jars and keep the olives unopened for 1 month before eating.

Makes 2 quarts

GRILLED BELL PEPPERS IN VINEGAR

These peppers make a perfect first course. Drizzle them with olive oil and add capers, anchovies, and parsley.

2½ to 3 pounds yellow bell peppers
2½ to 3 pounds red bell peppers
5 cups white wine vinegar
1 tablespoon salt
1 tablespoon coriander seeds
1 or 2 bay leaves

Broil the peppers in batches under a preheated broiler, turning them frequently, for 15 to 20 minutes, or until the skins are blistered and nearly black. Put the peppers in plastic bags, close the bags tight, and let the peppers cool until they can be easily handled. (This process loosens the skin and allows the peppers to continue to cook and soften.)

Set a sieve over a large bowl, hold each pepper over the sieve, and remove the skin. Break the peppers open and scrape away the seeds, allowing the juices to collect in the bowl. Discard the stem sections and pull the peppers apart in lengthwise segments along the natural ribs. Add the segments to the bowl of collected juices.

In a large nonreactive saucepan combine the peppers and juices, the vinegar, and salt. Bring the liquid to a boil and simmer the peppers for 10 minutes.

With a slotted spoon divide the peppers among warm jars up to 1 quart. Add a few coriander seeds and 1 bay leaf to each jar.

Boil the vinegar mixture over high heat for about 10 minutes or until it is reduced by half. Cover the peppers with the vinegar mixture, seal the jars, and process them in a boiling water bath: 10 minutes for jars up to 1 pint, 15 minutes for jars up to 1 quart. Let the jars cool completely before checking the seals and storing.

Makes 1½ quarts

RED SHALLOT MARMALADE

This marmalade makes an excellent sauce, hot or cold, for grilled meats and poultry.

3 pounds large red shallots, thinly sliced
⅓ cup extra-virgin olive oil
1 tablespoon salt
¾ cup sugar
¾ cup dry red wine
¾ cup red wine vinegar
½ teaspoon ground allspice

In a large nonreactive saucepan cook the shallots in the oil over low heat for 15 minutes, or until softened. Stir in the salt and sugar and cook the mixture, stirring frequently, for 15 minutes.

Add the wine and vinegar and bring the liquid to a boil. Simmer the marmalade, stirring frequently, for 30 minutes, or until it is thickened. Stir in the allspice and taste for seasoning.

Ladle the marmalade into four warm 1-cup jars and seal. Process the jars in a boiling water bath for 10 minutes. Let the jars cool completely before checking the seals and storing.

Makes 1 quart

A Mediterranean-style picnic can be quickly assembled from Green Olives in Brine, Grilled Peppers in Vinegar, and Wild Mushrooms in Oil.

GARLIC PUREE

Garlic purée is best when made with spring garlic—the young bulbs are moist and sweet—with green stalks. Spread the purée on croutons for soups, or use it in salad dressings or in almost any recipe calling for finely chopped garlic.

20 heads of young, tender garlic, whole and unpeeled
½ cup extra-virgin olive oil

Divide the garlic into 2 groups of 10 heads each, wrap each group in heavy-duty foil, and bake the garlic on a baking sheet in a preheated 375° oven for about 1 hour, or until the heads are very soft to the touch. Unwrap the garlic and let it cool until it can be handled.

Separate the garlic cloves from the heads and press each clove between the thumb and forefinger, squeezing the flesh into a sieve set over a bowl and discarding the papery coating. Force the garlic through the sieve into the bowl and stir in all but 2 tablespoons of the oil. Pack the purée into a sterilized 1-pint jar, top it with the remaining 2 tablespoons oil, and seal the jar. Once opened, keep a layer of olive oil on top.

Makes 1 pint

A section of an allotment garden in County Durham.

RED PEPPER SAUCE

Red bell peppers can be grilled and transformed into a soup base or a simple sauce for vegetables and pasta.

16 large red bell peppers
¼ cup red wine vinegar
¾ cup extra-virgin olive oil
2 tablespoons salt

Broil the peppers in batches under a preheated broiler, turning them frequently, for 15 to 20 minutes, or until the skins are blistered and nearly black. Put the peppers in plastic bags, close the bags tight, and let the peppers cool until they can be easily handled. (This process loosens the skin and allows the peppers to continue to cook and soften.)

Set a sieve over a large bowl, hold each pepper over the sieve, and remove the skin. Break the peppers open and scrape away the seeds, allowing the juices to collect in the bowl. Discard the stem sections and pull the peppers apart in lengthwise segments along the natural ribs. Add the segments to the bowl of collected juices.

Purée the peeled peppers with any accumulated juices in a blender or food processor and with the motor running add the vinegar, oil, and salt.

Ladle the purée into three sterilized 1-cup jars and seal. Process them in a boiling water bath for 10 minutes. Let the jars cool completely before checking the seals and storing. (Or divide the sauce among 1-cup freezer containers.)

Makes 1½ pints

RED PEPPER SOUP

4 shallots, thinly sliced
1 potato, thinly sliced
Salt
2 tablespoons olive oil
1 cup Red Pepper Sauce (page 189)
2 cups chicken stock
1 cup light cream
Cayenne pepper
About ¼ cup Sweet Basil Purée
   (page 221)

In a large skillet cook the shallots and the potato with a pinch of salt in the oil over low heat, stirring frequently, for 20 minutes, or until the vegetables are softened but not browned.

Add the red pepper sauce and the chicken stock and simmer the mixture for 10 minutes.

Purée the soup in a blender or food processor, transfer it to a saucepan, and whisk in the cream. Add the cayenne pepper and salt to taste.

Divide the soup among 4 soup bowls and spoon a generous tablespoon of the basil purée onto each serving.

Makes 4 cups

PUMPKIN PUREE

This unsweetened purée can be frozen and used in any recipe requiring canned pumpkin purée. It is ideal as a base for soups—such as Pumpkin and Spinach Soup (page 193)—pies, cakes, or savory gratins.

8- to 10-pound pumpkin

Quarter the pumpkin vertically, discard the stringy membranes, and, if you like, reserve the seeds for another use, such as roasting with coarse salt.

Put the pumpkin quarters in a deep roasting pan and add just enough water to come ½ inch up the sides of the pan. Bake the pumpkin, covered with foil, in a preheated 325° oven for about 1 hour and 15 minutes, or until it is tender when pierced with a fork, and let it cool, uncovered.

When the pumpkin is cool enough to handle, scoop out the flesh and purée it in a food mill or food processor. Pack the purée in convenient-to-use containers and freeze it.

Makes 6 to 7 cups

A fall harvest of pumpkins, along with garlic, shallots, and onions set out for drying.

191

PUMPKIN AND SPINACH SOUP

1 leek, washed well and thinly sliced
    into rounds
1 rib of celery, thinly sliced
2 tablespoons olive oil
2 cups frozen Pumpkin Purée (page
    191), thawed
3 cups chicken stock
⅛ teaspoon freshly grated nutmeg
Salt and freshly ground pepper
3 medium potatoes, boiled, peeled,
    and sliced into ¼-inch rounds
½ pound fresh spinach leaves, cut into
    thick ribbons
½ cup heavy cream

In a large saucepan cook the leek and celery in the oil over low heat, stirring frequently, for 10 minutes, or until they are softened.

Add the pumpkin purée, stock, nutmeg, and salt and pepper to taste. Bring the mixture to a boil and simmer it for 20 minutes. Purée the soup in a food processor or food mill and return it to the pan.

Add the potatoes and spinach and cook the mixture for 5 minutes, or until the vegetables are heated through. Taste for seasoning. Stir in the cream and ladle the soup into individual bowls.

Serves 6

Frozen pumpkin purée
makes an ideal base for a
hearty winter soup.

OLD-FASHIONED SQUASH PICKLES

These pickles will taste best if you use small, firm zucchini or yellow squash. The overgrown specimens lack concentrated flavor and will only exude more water during the salting period.

    6 pounds zucchini or yellow squash, or
      a mixture of both
    2 pounds red onions, thinly sliced
    1 cup coarse sea salt
    1 cup sugar
    2 teaspoons turmeric
    1 quart white wine vinegar
    2 teaspoons mustard seeds
    4 teaspoons coriander seeds

Slice the squash on the diagonal into ½-inch pieces. In a large bowl toss the squash with the onions and ¼ cup of the salt, cover the bowl, and let the vegetables sweat for 24 hours. Rinse the vegetables in a large basin of cold water and drain them immediately on a kitchen towel.

In a large enamel or other nonreactive saucepan combine the remaining ¾ cup salt, the sugar, and the turmeric. Stir in the vinegar slowly to make a smooth mixture, and heat the mixture over low heat, stirring, until the sugar is dissolved. Bring the mixture to a boil and boil it for 5 minutes. Remove the pan from the heat.

Add the drained vegetables and the mustard and coriander seeds. Let the mixture stand, uncovered, for at least 1 hour.

Bring the mixture to a boil over low heat. With a slotted spoon divide the vegetables among warm sterilized jars. Boil the liquid in the pan for 10 to 15 minutes, or until it is reduced by about 1 cup.

Ladle the boiling liquid into the jars, seal the jars immediately, and let the pickles cool. Store the unopened jars in a cool, dark place for 3 to 4 weeks before eating.

Makes 4 quarts

SUN-DRIED TOMATOES

Unless you live in a Mediterranean climate with brilliant sunshine, it's best not to fuss with drying tomatoes. Although friends claim that the oven method is suitable, I have yet to appreciate the results. However, you can preserve store-bought sun-dried tomatoes in oil and use them as is or purée them, both of which can be very satisfying and economical.

For tomatoes in oil, soak sun-dried tomatoes in a mixture of equal quantities of vinegar and water and let them soak for about 2 hours, or long enough to soften. Lift the tomatoes from the liquid and drain them on paper towels. Pat the tomatoes dry and pack them into sterilized jars. To each jar add a bay leaf, a dried chili or two, a good-quality extra-virgin olive oil to cover, seal the jars, and keep the tomatoes unopened for 2 to 3 days. The tomatoes keep for about 6 months.

To make a purée, process sun-dried tomatoes preserved in olive oil in a food processor or blender until smooth. If you like, add some fresh garlic and black pepper before serving. Store in sterilized jars with a coating of olive oil on top.

*Zucchini in flower in the
kitchen garden at
Northcut, Isle of Wight.*

LINGUINE WITH RED CLAM SAUCE

1 quart Tomatoes Preserved in
   Tomato Sauce (at night)
¼ cup extra-virgin olive oil
2 shallots, minced
1 garlic clove, minced
1 pound fresh baby clams, scrubbed
½ cup dry white wine
1 pound linguine
Salt and freshly ground pepper
½ cup minced flat-leaf parsley

In a large sauté pan gently cook the tomatoes and their sauce until they are heated through. Set aside.

In a deep saucepan heat the oil over moderate heat and in it cook the shallots and garlic until they are softened but not browned. Add the clams and white wine, bring the liquid to a boil, and cook the clams, covered, over moderate heat, shaking the pan from time to time, for 5 to 7 minutes, or until all the clams are opened. Set aside.

Cook the pasta in a large pan of boiling salted water until it is al dente and drain it.

Toss the pasta with the tomatoes in the sauté pan, add the clams and their cooking liquid, and season with salt and pepper to taste. Sprinkle the pasta with the parsley and serve immediately.

Serves 4

*A comforting dish of
Linguine with Red Clam
Sauce is particularly
special with homemade
Tomatoes Preserved in
Tomato Sauce.*

TOMATOES PRESERVED IN TOMATO SAUCE

12 pounds firm-ripe tomatoes,
   preferably plum
2 tablespoons salt
½ cup extra-virgin olive oil
1 onion, minced
2 garlic cloves, crushed
1 Bouquet Garni (page 237)
4 or 5 sprigs of fresh basil

Remove the core and slit an X in the skin at the base (blossom end) of 7 pounds of the tomatoes. Blanch the prepared tomatoes in a large saucepan of boiling salted water for 30 seconds, or until the skins split, drain them, and let them cool. When the tomatoes are cool enough to handle, peel and halve them (lengthwise for plum tomatoes and crosswise for rounder ones) and discard the seeds. Arrange the tomatoes in one layer in 1 or 2 large colanders set over a bowl or bowls, sprinkle them with 1 tablespoon of the salt, and let drain for several hours.

While the tomatoes are draining, in a large saucepan heat the oil over low heat and in it cook the onion and garlic until they are softened. Quarter the remaining 5 pounds tomatoes, add them to the pan with the bouquet garni, and cook the mixture over moderate heat for 25 to 30 minutes, or until they are softened. Discard the bouquet garni and force the tomato mixture through a sieve set over a bowl. Season the tomato sauce with the remaining 1 tablespoon salt and let it cool.

Pack the drained tomato halves in four or five 1-quart jars, add a sprig of fresh basil to each jar, and add enough sauce to cover the tomato halves.

Process the jars in a cold water bath for 45 minutes. Let the jars cool completely before checking the seals and storing.

Makes 4 or 5 quarts

POLENTA GRATIN
WITH PRESERVED TOMATOES
AND FONTINA

This preparation is a good example of how quickly a meal can be put together if you have preserved tomatoes on hand. The polenta can be prepared one day in advance to speed up the final preparation.

1 teaspoon coarse salt
1 cup coarse yellow cornmeal
2 tablespoons unsalted butter, softened
¼ cup extra-virgin olive oil plus additional oil for drizzling
2 cups Tomatoes Preserved in Tomato Sauce (page 197)
8 ounces Fontina, grated
Salt and freshly ground pepper

In a large saucepan bring 3 cups water to a boil with the salt. Gradually whisk in the cornmeal and cook the mixture over low heat, stirring constantly to prevent sticking and scorching, for 20 minutes, or until a solid mass forms. Beat in the butter.

Turn the mixture into a buttered 8 x 8 x 1½-inch pan and cover the surface with wax paper to prevent a crust from forming. Let the polenta cool for 1 hour. The polenta may be prepared up to 1 day in advance and kept covered.

Invert the polenta onto a cutting board and brush it with 2 tablespoons of the oil. Cut the polenta into 2-inch squares, halve the squares diagonally into triangles, and broil the triangles under a preheated broiler for 2 minutes, or until the tops are golden. Turn the triangles over, brush them with the remaining 2 tablespoons oil, and broil them until the tops are golden.

Arrange half the polenta triangles in a buttered gratin dish, spread half the tomatoes and sauce over the triangles, and top it with the remaining polenta. Spread the remaining tomatoes and sauce over the polenta and top them with the Fontina.

Season with salt and pepper to taste.

Bake the gratin in a preheated 400° oven for 10 minutes. Reduce the heat to 350° and continue baking until the tomatoes are hot and the cheese is melted and bubbling. If desired, drizzle the additional oil over the cheese. Serve immediately.

Serves 4 to 6

FRESH TUNA
WITH PRESERVED TOMATOES
IN TOMATO SAUCE

I first had tuna prepared this way in Italy. Although the tomatoes were fresh then, I find that the preparation is equally good with home-preserved ones.

2- to 2½-pound piece of fresh tuna, skinned
2 onions, thinly sliced
1 pound carrots, sliced into ½-inch rounds
2 garlic cloves, crushed
1 bay leaf
A few sprigs of fresh thyme
1 cup extra-virgin olive oil
1 quart Tomatoes Preserved in Tomato Sauce (page 197)
Salt and freshly ground pepper

In a large, shallow, flameproof baking dish combine the tuna, onions, carrots, garlic, bay leaf, thyme, and ½ cup of the oil and let the mixture marinate at room temperature for 30 minutes.

Cover the tuna with the remaining oil and the tomatoes with sauce. Bring the liquid to a boil over low heat and then bake the tuna mixture, covered with foil, in a preheated 350° oven for 1 hour. Remove the foil and continue cooking the tuna mixture, basting frequently, for 30 minutes, or until the tuna is tender. Let the tuna cool at room temperature.

Spoon as much of the sauce as you can into a bowl and check it for seasoning, adding salt and pepper to taste. Slice the tuna diagonally as thin as possible, arrange it on a platter, and spoon the sauce and vegetables over the tuna.

Serves 8 to 10

GREEN TOMATO CHUTNEY

This is an absolutely classic English specialty—and a very straightforward way to preserve autumn's lingering green tomatoes.

6 pounds green tomatoes
4 tablespoons salt
2 pounds cooking apples, peeled, cored, and coarsely chopped
1 pound red onions, thinly sliced
4 shallots, minced
3 to 4 garlic cloves, minced, or pounded to a paste with a little salt in a mortar with a pestle
2 teaspoons freshly grated ginger
2 cups red wine vinegar
2 Dried Hot Chilies (page 225)
1 teaspoon cuminseed
3 whole cloves
¼ cup dry mustard
1½ cups firmly packed dark brown sugar
1½ cups dried currants

Remove the core and slit an X in the skin at the base (blossom end) of the tomatoes. Blanch the tomatoes in a large saucepan of boiling salted water for 1 minute and drain them in a colander. When the tomatoes are cool enough to handle, peel and halve them crosswise and discard the seeds. Chop the flesh into ½-inch pieces, toss it with 2 tablespoons of the salt, and let it drain in a colander for 2 hours.

In a large enamel or other nonreactive saucepan combine the drained tomatoes, the apples, red onions, shallots, garlic, gin-

ger, the remaining 2 tablespoons salt, and 1 cup of the vinegar. Bring the mixture to a boil over low heat and simmer it, stirring frequently, for 30 minutes.

While the tomato mixture is cooking, in a spice or coffee grinder grind the chilies, cuminseed, and cloves to a fine powder. In a bowl combine the chili mixture with the mustard and the brown sugar.

Add the remaining 1 cup vinegar, the spice mixture, and the currants to the tomato mixture and simmer the chutney, stirring frequently, for 45 minutes, or until it is reduced by about one-fourth.

Spoon the chutney into warm sterilized jars and seal. Store the unopened jars in a cool, dark place for at least 3 months before eating.

Makes 2 quarts

199

RICH TOMATO SAUCE

Little effort is required to preserve the fresh flavor of summer tomatoes.

¼ cup extra-virgin olive oil
1 large onion, finely chopped
2 carrots, finely chopped
6 pounds ripe tomatoes (preferably
    plum), blanched for 1 minute in
    boiling water, peeled, seeded, and
    coarsely chopped
1 head of garlic, whole and unpeeled
1 Bouquet Garni (page 237)
2 tablespoons coarse salt

In a large saucepan heat the oil over low heat and in it cook the onion and carrots for about 20 minutes, or until they are softened. Add the tomatoes and garlic, bouquet garni, and salt. Bring the mixture to a boil over moderate heat and simmer it, uncovered, for 45 minutes.

Discard the bouquet garni and strain the sauce through a medium-meshed sieve into a bowl, pressing hard on the solids to extract all the juices. Return the mixture to the pan and reheat the sauce until it just starts to bubble. Taste for seasoning.

Ladle the sauce into warm jars and process in a boiling water bath: 30 minutes for jars up to 1 pint, 45 minutes for jars up to 1 quart. Let the jars cool completely before checking the seals and storing.

Makes 2 quarts

Ribbons of homemade pasta—plain and flavored with beet purée and spinach—are left to dry before cooking.

TOMATO KETCHUP

You will never feel guilty reaching for a bottle of homemade ketchup. The pure tomato flavor of this sauce is incomparable.

10 pounds ripe tomatoes, peeled,
    seeded, and coarsely chopped
3 red bell peppers, coarsely chopped
4 large red onions, thinly sliced
1 head of garlic, whole and unpeeled
2 cups red wine vinegar
1 cup firmly packed brown sugar
2 teaspoons coarse salt
1 tablespoon celery seeds
¼-inch-thick slice of fresh ginger
1 small piece of blade mace
1 tablespoon mustard seeds
2 teaspoons black peppercorns

In a large nonreactive pan combine the tomatoes, bell peppers, onions, garlic, and 1 cup of the vinegar. Bring the liquid to a boil and simmer the mixture for 25 minutes, or until all the vegetables are softened and can be crushed against the side of the pan with a wooden spoon.

Remove and discard the garlic and purée the vegetables in a food processor or food mill. Return the purée to the pan and add the remaining 1 cup vinegar, the brown sugar, and salt. Add all the spices, tied up in a cheesecloth bag. Bring the liquid to a boil and simmer the mixture, stirring frequently, for 2 hours, or until it is very thick.

Taste the ketchup for seasoning. Ladle into four warm 1-pint jars and seal. Process the jars in a boiling water bath for 10 minutes. Let the jars cool completely before checking the seals and storing.

Makes 2 quarts

Left: Tomatoes ripening on the vine. Above: Rows of onions drying.

GREEN VEGETABLE CHUTNEY

This is a wonderful recipe for transforming the last of the summer's green beans, green tomatoes, and green bell peppers into a lasting memory. Enjoy this chutney as an accompaniment to a simple sandwich of farmhouse Cheddar.

5 pounds green tomatoes
1 tablespoon salt
3 pounds green bell peppers
1 pound green beans
¼ cup extra-virgin olive oil
4 onions, thinly sliced
3 to 4 garlic cloves, minced
3 small Dried Hot Chilies (page 225)
1 bay leaf
¼ teaspoon saffron threads, dissolved
   in 1 tablespoon boiling-hot water
1 cup firmly packed dark brown sugar
½ cup granulated sugar
3 cups white wine vinegar
1 cup dried currants
4 tablespoons coriander seeds, ground

Blanch the tomatoes in a large pan of boiling water for 1 minute, and transfer them with a slotted spoon to a colander to drain, reserving the water for the bell peppers. When the tomatoes are cool enough to handle, peel and slice them in half crosswise and discard the seeds. Chop the pulp into ½-inch pieces, toss it with the salt, and let it drain in a colander for 2 hours.

Cut the bell peppers into ½-inch pieces. Bring the reserved water to a boil, in it blanch the bell pepper pieces for 5 minutes, and transfer them to a colander to drain, reserving the water for the beans.

Slice the beans on the diagonal into ½-inch lengths. Bring the reserved water to a boil, in it blanch the beans for 1 minute, and drain them.

In a deep enamel or other large heavy saucepan heat the oil over low heat, add the onions, garlic, chilies, bay leaf, and saffron mixture, and cook the mixture, covered, for 10 to 15 minutes, or until the onions are softened. While the mixture is cooking, in a small saucepan cook the brown and granulated sugars with the vinegar over low heat, stirring, until they are dissolved.

Discard the chilies and bay leaf, add the blanched green vegetables, the currants, ground coriander, and sugar and vinegar mixture. Bring the chutney to a boil over medium heat and simmer it, stirring frequently, particularly at the end, for 1 hour, or until it is quite thick.

Spoon the chutney into warm sterilized jars and seal. Store the unopened jars in a cool, dark place for at least 3 months before eating.

Makes 2½ quarts

MIXED VEGETABLE SALAD

The selection of vegetables in this preparation can vary according to seasonal availability and personal taste. Mushrooms, leeks, fennel, celery, and many others can all be used. The vegetables are perfect as a simple first course: serve with a little of the sauce and sprinkle with chopped herbs.

4 zucchini, cut into ¼-inch rounds
1 pound thin green beans
2 heads of cauliflower, broken into
   flowerets
4 red bell peppers, cut into ½-inch-
   wide lengthwise strips
1 pound asparagus, cut diagonally into
   ½-inch pieces
1 pound small boiling onions, peeled
2 bunches of small whole carrots,
   peeled
About 2 cups coarse sea salt
6 cups white wine vinegar
4 cups extra-virgin olive oil
4 to 8 Dried Hot Chilies (page 225)
2 tablespoons dill seed
4 bay leaves

Reweigh all the prepared vegetables and in a large bowl or stoneware crock combine them with ¼ cup coarse sea salt and 2 cups water for every 1 pound vegetables. Let the vegetables soak for at least 12 hours or overnight. Drain the vegetables, rinse them in cold water, and drain them again.

In a large pan bring the vinegar to a boil and add the vegetables (if the pan is not large enough, do this in batches). Bring the vinegar back to a boil and cook the vegetables for 5 minutes, then with a slotted spoon transfer them to a large bowl.

Boil the vinegar over high heat until it is reduced to about 4 cups. Add the oil, boil for a few minutes, and let it cool slightly.

Arrange the vegetables attractively in four warm sterilized 1-quart jars. Divide the chilies, dill seed, and bay leaves among the jars.

Pour the oil and vinegar mixture over the vegetables and seal the jars. Store the unopened jars in a cool, dark place for at least 2 weeks before eating.

Makes 1 gallon

A bed of nasturtiums at Clapham House, Sussex.

FLOWER PERFUMED VINEGAR

Flowers such as lavender, nasturtiums, elder flowers, and violets can be used to delicately flavor vinegars. The process requires that the flowers be left to macerate in the vinegar for a couple of months.

Before proceeding, any dirt or dust should be removed from the fresh flowers and the flowers spread out on a drying rack for 1 day, preferably in the sunlight, to concentrate the flavors. The flowers are then ready for use on their own or in combination with other aromatics to flavor vinegar. Of all the types of vinegar, wine vinegars, particularly red wine vinegar, lend themselves best to flavoring.

The following procedure is a rough guide for all flower-perfumed vinegars. Vary the additional aromatics to suit your own taste.

2 large handfuls of fresh flowers, left to
   dry overnight
1 head of garlic, excess "papery"
   coatings discarded
2 to 3 shallots, crushed
2 teaspoons whole cloves
2 quarts red wine vinegar

Combine the flowers, garlic, shallots, and cloves in a 3- to 4-quart nonreactive container (glazed stoneware is generally best, as it does not absorb or emit flavors).

Bring the vinegar to a boil in a saucepan and pour it over the dry ingredients. When the vinegar is cool, cover the container and allow the mixture to mellow for 2 months.

Strain the mixture through a sieve lined with a double thickness of dampened cheesecloth. Transfer the vinegar to bottles and seal.

Makes 2 quarts

RHUBARB AND ROSE PETAL JAM

This is a lovely jam with a scent of roses and delicate rhubarb flavor. Old-fashioned roses add a more prominent note but ordinary garden varieties can be used.

4 pounds tender fresh rhubarb
5 cups sugar
½ cup Apple Pectin Stock (page 63) or
    2 cooking apples, peeled, cored, and finely chopped, the seeds reserved in a cheesecloth bag
¼ cup fresh lemon juice
1½ to 2 cups red rose petals, with the white heel of each petal trimmed and discarded

Slice the rhubarb crosswise into ½-inch pieces and layer it with the sugar in a large bowl. (If you are using the cooking apples, layer them, including the seeds, with the rhubarb and sugar.) Let the mixture stand, covered, for at least 12 hours.

Tip the contents of the bowl (including the cheesecloth bag of seeds) into a preserving pan and bring the liquid to a boil over low heat. Add the pectin stock (if fresh apples were not used earlier) and the lemon juice and boil the mixture, skimming any froth from the surface, for 20 minutes, or, until the jelling point is reached. Discard the bag of apple seeds and let the jam cool for 10 minutes.

Stir in the rose petals, ladle the jam into warm sterilized jars, and seal.

Makes 1½ quarts

Above: Tender stalks of rhubarb in the morning sun. Overleaf: The kitchen garden at Barnsley House, Gloucestershire, is neatly organized into well defined sections with herbaceous borders and ornamental rose bushes.

FLOWER-SCENTED SUGARS

Flavored sugars take only minutes to prepare, yet their shelf life is limitless, providing they are properly stored. Once the sugar is perfumed, it can be used to add a special note to pastry doughs, custards, ice creams, cakes, cookies, and even jellies.

The most aromatic flowers to use are lavender, roses, and violets. Sweet geranium leaves and lemon balm leaves are also good to use. Make sure that the flavorings you collect are dry. Shake off any dust and foreign particles (try to avoid picking any flowers that would necessitate washing). Flowers should be trimmed of the white heel, which can be bitter, and the leaves should be slightly crushed to increase the diffusion of flavor. Leave the flavorings spread out in a single layer on a wire drying rack overnight; this will help concentrate flavor.

For every 4 cups sugar, use either ½ cup petals, several branches of lavender, or 3 or 4 geranium or lemon balm leaves. Layer the ingredients in a storage jar and leave for at least 2 weeks to allow for the transfer of flavor. The flavorings can then be sifted from the sugar and discarded or left in the jar as a pleasant reminder of the flavor.

LAVENDER ICE CREAM

Lavender ice cream is a wonderfully subtle end to a meal. It is easily prepared by infusing the milk to be used for making a simple vanilla ice cream with a few dried branches of lavender. Follow the directions for Vanilla Ice Cream (page 235) and replace the vanilla bean with 3 or 4 lavender branches. Allow the lavender to steep in the milk for 30 minutes before straining. To serve, sprinkle each portion with a few crumbled lavender buds.

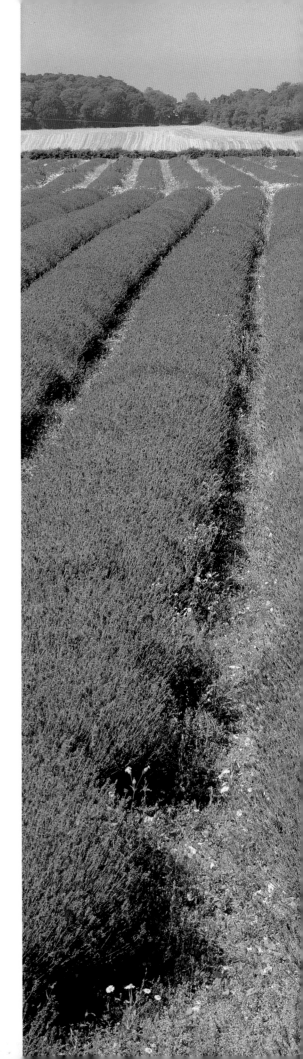

Fields of lavender in Norfolk with the sea beyond.

SORREL PUREE

Sorrel is a lemon-flavored leafy green. Somewhat neglected in America, in France sorrel is no more unusual than spinach and is used in abundance for soups, in egg dishes, and in sauces, particularly for oily fish such as salmon and shad.

The French varieties of sorrel grow exceedingly well, even if confined to a balcony pot. During the summer and autumn growing months, remove the leaves as soon as they develop. Use them fresh or freeze them for the winter months.

1 pound sorrel, washed and stemmed
½ stick (¼ cup) unsalted butter

Stack several sorrel leaves on top of one another and roll them lengthwise. Slice the bundle into thin ribbons. Continue with the remaining sorrel until it is all sliced.

In a large nonreactive saucepan heat the butter over low heat and in it cook the sorrel, stirring constantly, until it is completely wilted and forms a purée. Let it cool and pack it into a freezer container.

Makes ½ cup

SORREL SAUCE

1 cup heavy cream
½ cup frozen Sorrel Purée (above),
  thawed
1 to 2 tablespoons unsalted butter
Salt
Cayenne pepper

In a saucepan bring the cream to a boil. Whisk in the sorrel purée. Whisk in the butter. Season to taste with salt and cayenne pepper.

Makes 1½ cups

SORREL SOUP

4 scallions, thinly sliced
1 potato, thinly sliced
½ stick (¼ cup) butter
2 cups shredded lettuce (any green
　leafy type)
4 cups chicken stock
2 large eggs
Salt
½ cup frozen Sorrel Purée (page 219),
　thawed
½ cup heavy cream
Pinch of sugar
Cayenne pepper

In a large nonreactive saucepan cook the scallions and the potato in 3 tablespoons of the butter over a low heat, stirring frequently for about 10 minutes, or until the vegetables are softened but not browned. Add the lettuce and stock, bring the liquid just to a boil, and simmer for 20 minutes.

Meanwhile, beat the eggs in a bowl with a pinch of salt. Heat the remaining tablespoon butter in an 8-inch omelet pan over medium heat, add the eggs and lift up the edge in several places, tilting the pan, to allow the liquid to run underneath. Flip the omelet and cook it for 30 seconds or until slightly golden. Transfer to a cutting board.

Purée the soup mixture in a food processor with the sorrel purée and in the large saucepan heat the mixture with the cream, sugar, and salt and cayenne to taste over low heat until the soup is heated through.

Ladle the soup into 4 bowls. Cut the omelet into ¼-inch-wide ribbons and divide them among the bowls.

Serves 4

*Freshly picked sorrel from
Dunsborough Park,
Surrey. Overleaf: tender
spring vine leaves from a
London garden.*

SWEET BASIL PUREE

If you have a large bed of basil in your garden, this is a sensible and convenient method for preserving the flavor of the aromatic leaves at the end of summer. Sweet Greek and Italian basil varieties have the best flavor for preserving, whereas dark opal basil is best used fresh. Use 1 or 2 tablespoons of the purée in salad dressings, as an accompaniment to grilled fish and vegetables, steamed new potatoes, or, naturally, with pasta. Add freshly ground pine nuts, garlic, and grated Parmesan for a delicious pesto sauce. And a dollop of the basil purée will certainly add a cheery note to a bowl of vegetable or tomato soup.

5 cups packed stemmed, washed, and
　dried basil leaves (about 5 ounces)
2 tablespoons fine sea salt
1 cup extra-virgin olive oil plus
　additional oil for sealing the jars

In a blender combine the basil leaves with the salt. With the motor running, add 1 cup of oil in a thin stream. Scrape down the blender jar with a spatula from time to time and continue processing until the mixture is completely smooth.

Transfer the basil to small sterilized jars and pour a ⅛-inch layer of oil over each surface. It is best to pack the purée in amounts that will be used up soon after opening. To prevent discoloration after opening, pour an additional layer of oil over the remaining contents.

Makes 2½ cups

Preceding pages: Vine leaves for preserving. Above: Roast Quail in Vine Leaves.

PRESERVED VINE LEAVES

If you have access to a grape vine, even if the grapes are not suitable for table or wine, it is amusing to preserve the leaves for use throughout the year. They can give new life to leftovers by acting as a wrapping. Stuffed with a rice or meat filling, the little packages can be eaten cold as an hors d'oeuvre; if grilled or baked in a tomato sauce, they make a good first course. Preserved vine leaves are also useful when roasting small game birds. Cover the breast meat with a few leaves to keep the flesh succulent (see Roast Quail in Vine Leaves at right).

1 pound young tender vine leaves
1 cup coarse sea salt

Wash the vine leaves and carefully remove each stem without tearing the leaf. Plunge the leaves in 4 batches into a pan of boiling water, return the water to a boil, and transfer the leaves to paper towels or kitchen towels to drain.

Bring 2 quarts water to a boil and add the salt, stirring until the salt is dissolved.

Divide the leaves among four warm 1-pint jars. Pour about 2 cups of the boiling-hot brine into each jar and seal. Process the jars in a boiling water bath for 5 minutes. Let cool completely before checking the seals and storing. For any subsequent preparation, rinse the brine from the leaves under cold running water and pat the leaves dry.

Makes 2 quarts

224

ROAST QUAIL IN VINE LEAVES

Preserved vine leaves come in handy to protect breasts of small birds from drying out during roasting. Even though the bird may be the main attraction, the slightly browned and crispy vine leaves are also delicious. To serve, set each quail on a potato pancake or a 3-inch round crouton.

8 Preserved Vine Leaves (at left)
4 quails
Salt and freshly ground pepper
2 tablespoons unsalted butter,
   softened
2 tablespoons red wine vinegar
2 tablespoons red currant jelly or
   Rowanberry and Crabapple Jelly
   (page 155)
4 tablespoons heavy cream
Watercress leaves, for garnish

Rinse the vine leaves to remove excess salt and pat them dry with paper towels.

Sprinkle the cavities of the birds with some salt and pepper. Carefully cover the breast of each bird with 2 of the vine leaves and tie the legs together with trussing string. Rub the quails with 1 tablespoon of the butter.

In a roasting pan roast the quails in a preheated to 450° oven, basting every 10 minutes, for 30 minutes. Remove the quails from the oven and keep them warm.

Drain the excess fat from the roasting pan, add the vinegar and jelly, and cook the mixture over high heat, scraping up the browned bits. Whisk in the cream and taste for seasoning. Swirl in the remaining tablespoon of butter and strain the sauce into a small serving bowl.

Remove the strings from the quails. Set them on a platter and garnish with the watercress. Pass the sauce separately.

Serves 4

DRIED HOT CHILIES

Drying chilies concentrates their flavor and strength for use in subsequent preparations, such as soups, stews, and sauces. The chilies may be used whole for a potent effect or seeded for a milder taste.

Choose firm-ripe red chilies and wipe them clean with a damp cloth. String the chilies by threading their stems with a needle and kitchen string. Hang the chilies to dry in a warm dry area for 2 weeks, or until they have shriveled and are approximately half their original size.

Remove the chilies from the string and store them in a covered container to prevent their collecting dust.

HARISSA

Harissa is a very hot chili paste that is used as a condiment in Tunisia, mainly with the well-known couscous preparations. A tiny amount of the paste goes a long way in livening up a meat stew. If you like, mix a small amount of Garlic Purée (page 189) into the *harissa* before using.

½ pound Dried Hot Chilies (above),
   seeded (wear rubber gloves)
2 teaspoons caraway seeds
½ teaspoon salt
About ½ cup extra-virgin olive oil

In a saucepan soak the chilies in warm water to cover for 2 hours. Drain the chilies and pat them dry.

Grind the chilies with the caraway seeds and salt in a mortar with a pestle until combined well. Slowly blend in ½ cup oil to make a smooth thin paste, adding more oil if necessary. Transfer the *harissa* to a sterilized jar and seal the jar.

Makes 1 cup

KITCHEN SAMPLER

CREPES

If you are not preparing them ahead of time—crêpes keep quite well in the refrigerator or freezer—be sure to allow for the one hour that the batter must rest before you can make the crêpes.

1 cup milk
3 large eggs
¾ cup all-purpose flour
Pinch of salt
Pinch of brown sugar
1 stick (½ cup) plus 2 tablespoons
    unsalted butter, melted and cooled

In a large bowl whisk together the milk and eggs until they are just combined. Sift together the flour, salt, and brown sugar and whisk them gradually into the milk mixture. Stir in all of the melted butter and let the batter stand at room temperature for about 1 hour.

Heat an 8-inch crêpe pan or skillet and brush it with a little butter. Check the consistency of the batter; it should pour like heavy cream. If it is too thick add a little milk. Add 3 to 4 tablespoons of the batter to the hot pan, rotating the pan quickly to distribute the batter, and cook the crêpe for about 20 seconds, until the underside is golden. Flip the crêpe with a spatula, cook the other side and transfer the crêpe to a plate. Continue cooking crêpes in the same manner, stacking them on the plate. (The pan should not require additional butter, as there is a sufficient amount in the batter.)

Makes about 14 crêpes

Page 226: Blackberry
Jam Picnic Cake. Left:
Freshly made crêpes filled
with Fresh Fig and Vine
Ripened Grape Jam.

POUND CAKE

A true pound cake is made from four ingredients—butter, sugar, eggs, and flour—weighing one pound each, though here I've halved these amounts. No additional leavening agents are necessary if enough air is whisked into the butter, sugar, and egg mixture. To ensure accurate weight measurements, use a scale.

Sliced pound cake, fresh or toasted, can be transformed into a special teatime sweet when served with a fruit preserve. For dessert, a scoop of vanilla ice cream with a jam such as Chunky Vanilla Pear Jam (page 139) is hard to beat.

½ pound (2 sticks) unsalted butter, softened
Pinch of salt
½ pound superfine sugar
4 large eggs
½ pound all-purpose flour

In a large bowl cream the butter with the salt for 8 minutes, or until the butter is very pale. Slowly add the sugar, beating until it "melts" into the butter. Beat in the eggs, one at at time, making sure that each one is completely incorporated before the next is added. Fold the flour into the mixture in 3 batches, with a slotted spoon. (Do not overblend or the cake will be tough.)

Transfer the batter to a buttered and floured 9 x 4 x 3-inch loaf pan and make a lengthwise indention down the center of the batter with a spatula. Bake the cake in a preheated 350° oven for 45 minutes, or until a skewer inserted in the center comes out clean. Let the cake cool in the pan on a wire rack for 15 minutes, invert it onto the rack, and let it cool completely.

Makes one loaf cake

SCONES

The English tradition of scones served with homemade jam and whipped cream will always be a teatime favorite.

½ cup dried currants (optional)
2 cups all-purpose flour
1 tablespoon sugar
1 teaspoon baking soda
2 teaspoons cream of tartar
Salt
½ stick (¼ cup) unsalted butter, cut into bits
2 large eggs
1 cup buttermilk

If using the currants, plump them in hot water for 15 minutes. Drain them well.

Sift the flour, sugar, baking soda, cream of tartar, and a pinch of salt together into a large bowl. Rub the butter into the flour mixture until it is well incorporated and the mixture resembles coarse meal. Add the currants if desired.

Combine 1 of the eggs with the buttermilk in a bowl and stir the mixture into the flour mixture with a fork until the dough just forms a ball. Gently knead the dough on a floured surface for a few seconds, or until it is smooth. Shape it into a ¾-inch-thick round and cut out rounds with a 2½-inch floured cutter.

Transfer the rounds to a buttered baking sheet. In a small bowl beat the remaining egg with a pinch of salt and brush the egg mixture over the tops of the scones. Bake the scones in a preheated 425° oven for 10 to 12 minutes, or until they are golden. Serve the scones straight from the oven or warm.

Makes 10 to 12 scones

BASIC SPONGE CAKE

A basic sponge cake, or *génoise*, is made by beating whole eggs with sugar and folding in flour and melted butter. This cake can be transformed into a simple or elaborate creation with the addition of homemade preserves. It may be sliced into layers and reassembled with jam, jelly, or a fruit curd and dusted with confectioners' sugar. Or it may be baked in a jelly-roll pan and filled with preserved fruit, such as blackberries or raspberries. During the winter try a sweetened chestnut purée filling with a chocolate sauce. To make a chocolate *génoise*, substitute ¼ cup unsweetened cocoa powder for ¼ cup of the flour.

    4 large eggs
    ½ cup sugar
    ¾ cup sifted all-purpose flour
    ½ stick (¼ cup) unsalted butter,
        melted and cooled

In a large bowl set over simmering water, beat the eggs with the sugar for about 10 minutes, or until the mixture ribbons when the whisk is lifted. Remove the bowl from the simmering water and continue whisking (or beating) until the mixture is tripled in bulk and cooled.

Sift the flour over the egg mixture in 3 batches, folding it in gently but thoroughly with a slotted spoon and adding the butter with the last batch of flour.

Butter and flour a 9-inch round or square cake pan, or a 7- or 8-inch springform pan. Pour the batter into the prepared pan and bake it in a preheated to 350° oven for 30 to 35 minutes, or until the top is springy to the touch and the edges begin to pull away from the sides of the pan. Let the cake cool in the pan on a wire rack for 5 minutes, invert it onto the rack, and let it cool completely.

Makes a single
round or square layer

YOGURT BREAD

This is my "health" bread; the original recipe was given to me by my friend Caroline Jacobs, who has been spreading the word on her travels from South Africa to France, America, and England. The dense texture of this bread makes it delicious toasted and spread with any homemade jam or jelly.

    2 tablespoons honey
    2 cups natural whole-milk yogurt
    1 pound whole-wheat or mixed-grain
        flour
    1 teaspoon salt
    1 tablespoon baking soda
    ½ cup wheat berries plus additional for
        sprinkling the bread

Combine the honey and yogurt in a bowl and let the mixture stand for 5 to 10 minutes, or until the honey "dissolves."

In a large bowl combine the remaining ingredients, make a well in the center, and add the yogurt mixture. Gradually draw the dry ingredients into the well with a wooden spoon and continue to stir until the dough forms a ball. Knead the dough on a floured surface for a few minutes; the dough will not become smooth and shiny like most bread doughs.

Transfer the dough to a buttered loaf pan, about 9 x 4 x 3 inches. Make a lengthwise indentation down the center with a spatula, and sprinkle the bread with additional wheat berries. Bake the bread in a preheated 425° oven for 15 minutes. Lower the heat to 350° and continue baking for 1 hour more.

Unmold the bread, lower the heat to 325°, and bake the bread for 15 minutes more, or until the bottom sounds hollow when tapped.

Makes 1 loaf

Fresh green almonds and small almond cakes, called visitandines, are served with Pitted Cherries in Almond Syrup.

VISITANDINES

Visitandines are small barquette-shaped almond cakes. The best flavor comes from using good-quality almonds and fresh sweet butter. The almond cakes can be baked and stored for a few days in an airtight container, although they are at their peak when they are straight out of the oven. Serve the visitandines as an accompaniment to bottled fruits, particularly Spirited Morello Cherries (page 88) and Whole Apricots in Vanilla Syrup (page 69).

¾ stick (6 tablespoons) unsalted butter
    plus 3 tablespoons, melted, for
    brushing the molds
⅓ cup all-purpose flour
¾ cup confectioners' sugar
1 cup freshly ground blanched almonds
3 large egg whites

Generously brush 25 barquette molds (about 1-tablespoon capacity each) with the 3 tablespoons melted butter.

In a small saucepan heat the remaining ¾ stick butter over moderate heat until it just starts to brown. Remove from the heat.

Sift the flour with the confectioners' sugar into a saucepan and add the almonds. Whisk the egg whites into the mixture and heat it over low heat, whisking continuously, until it is just warm. Remove the pan from the heat and stir in the browned butter.

Pour the batter to within ¼ inch of the prepared molds on a baking sheet and bake the cakes in a preheated 425° oven for 10 to 15 minutes, or until the tops are slightly cracked and springy to the touch. Unmold and let the cakes cool rightside up on a rack.

Makes 25 small cakes

BUCKWHEAT PANCAKES

These pancakes are particularly good served with Pure Apple Butter with Cardamon (page 66) or Blackberry Purée (page 151) and apple wedges sautéed in butter.

    1½ cups all-purpose flour
    ½ cup buckwheat flour
    1 teaspoon baking soda
    ½ teaspoon salt
    2 large eggs
    1 tablespoon honey
    ½ stick (¼ cup) unsalted butter, melted and cooled, plus additional melted butter for brushing the griddle
    1 to 1½ cups buttermilk

Sift the dry ingredients together into a bowl and make a well in the center. In another bowl beat the eggs with the honey, the ¼ cup melted butter, and 1 cup of the buttermilk and add the mixture to the well. Gradually draw the dry ingredients into the center with a fork, adding the remaining ½ cup buttermilk if necessary to make a smooth batter. (Do not overblend.)

Heat a pancake griddle or skillet (preferably nonstick) over moderate heat, brush it lightly with some of the additional butter, and make pancakes using ¼ cup of batter at a time. When bubbles appear on the surface and the undersides are brown, flip the pancakes over with a metal spatula and brown the other side. Keep the cooked pancakes warm in a low oven while making the rest.

Makes about ten 4-inch pancakes

WAFFLES

Waffles are simple to prepare and a great companion for homemade fruit syrups or sauces, such as Whole Blueberry Sauce (page 77), or jams and fruit butters.

    2 cups all-purpose flour
    2 teaspoons baking powder
    1 teaspoon baking soda
    ¼ teaspoon salt
    2 teaspoons sugar
    2 large eggs
    1½ cups buttermilk
    ½ stick (¼ cup) unsalted butter, melted and cooled

Sift the dry ingredients together into a bowl and make a well in the center. In another bowl beat the eggs with the buttermilk and butter and add the mixture to the well. Gradually draw the dry ingredients into the center with a fork to make a smooth batter. (Do not overblend the batter, or the waffles will be heavy.)

Heat a waffle iron without any fat and ladle enough batter into the center to spread out and cover about two-thirds of the surface. Cover the batter with the lid and leave the lid closed for about 4 minutes or until the steaming stops. Transfer the waffle to a heated plate and keep it warm in a low oven while making the rest.

Makes six to eight 6½-inch waffles

BASIC SHORTCRUST DOUGH

8-INCH TART:
1 cup all-purpose flour
½ teaspoon salt
½ stick (¼ cup) unsalted butter, cut into bits
1 large egg yolk
2 to 3 tablespoons cold water

12-INCH TART:
2 cups all-purpose flour
1 teaspoon salt
1 stick (½ cup) unsalted butter, cut into bits
2 large egg yolks
4 to 5 tablespoons cold water

In a large bowl combine the flour and salt. Rub the butter into the flour mixture until it is well incorporated and the mixture resembles coarse meal.

In a bowl beat the egg yolk(s) with the cold water and add the mixture to the flour mixture, stirring until the dough forms a ball. Wrap the dough in wax paper and chill it for at least 15 minutes before rolling it out.

PASTRY CREAM

Pastry cream and fruit are a very complementary pairing. For a simple dessert, spread pastry cream in a prebaked pastry shell and top it with preserved fruits, such as apricots, cherries, or peaches. If you like, flavor the cream with some of the preserving syrup.

  2 cups milk
  1 vanilla bean, split lengthwise
  6 large egg yolks
  ½ cup sugar
  3 tablespoons all-purpose flour

In a saucepan scald the milk with the vanilla bean over low heat and let the mixture stand, covered, for 10 minutes.

In a bowl beat the yolks with the sugar until the mixture is light and fluffy. Beat in the flour.

Discard the vanilla bean and slowly whisk the milk into the yolk mixture. Transfer the mixture to the pan, cook it over low heat, whisking frequently, until the sauce bubbles and thickens, and cook it for about 2 minutes more.

Transfer the pastry cream to a bowl, cover the surface with a piece of plastic wrap or the paper from a stick of butter, and let the pastry cream cool.

Makes 2 cups

SWEET RICH PASTRY DOUGH

8- TO 10-INCH TART:
1 cup all-purpose flour
¼ teaspoon salt
3 tablespoons sugar
½ stick (¼ cup) unsalted butter, cut into bits
2 large egg yolks

10- TO 12-INCH TART:
1½ cups all-purpose flour
½ teaspoon salt
⅓ cup sugar
¾ stick (6 tablespoons) unsalted butter, cut into bits
3 large egg yolks

In a large bowl combine the flour, salt, and sugar. Rub the butter into the flour mixture until it is well incorporated and the mixture resembles coarse meal.

In a bowl beat the egg yolks until they are just combined and add them to the flour mixture, stirring until the dough forms a ball. Wrap the dough in wax paper and chill it for at least 15 minutes before rolling it out.

SIMPLE SUGAR SYRUPS

These guidelines are for making simple sugar syrups, ranging in density from light to heavy. Use whichever density suits your taste or the fruit being preserved.

LIGHT: 2 cups sugar, 4 cups water,
2 tablespoons fresh lemon juice

MEDIUM: 2 cups sugar, 2 cups water,
1 tablespoon fresh lemon juice

HEAVY: 2 cups sugar, 1 cup water,
1 tablespoon fresh lemon juice

Heat the sugar, water, and lemon juice in a saucepan. Stirring over low heat, until the sugar is dissolved. Increase the heat to moderate and boil the syrup for 1 minute.

Makes 1½ to 5 cups

FRUIT SORBETS

Fruit sorbets consist of a simple sugar syrup blended with a fruit purée. Raspberry and black currant are my particular favorites.

1 cup sugar
2 tablespoons fresh lemon juice
1 cup unsweetened fruit purée

In a saucepan heat the sugar with 2 cups water over low heat, stirring frequently, until the sugar dissolves. Bring the syrup to a boil, boil it for 1 minute, and cool.

Stir the lemon juice and fruit purée into the syrup and chill the mixture for at least 1 hour.

Transfer the mixture to an ice cream machine and freeze it according to the manufacturer's instructions. The sorbet can be stored in the freezer, but the flavor and texture is always best straight from the machine.

Makes 1 quart

VANILLA ICE CREAM

Homemade vanilla ice cream is hard to improve upon except with the addition of fruit, puréed or whole. The fruit can be added to the chilled custard and then churned. For a swirled effect, a purée can be added just as the ice cream is set. If the purée is unsweetened, sweeten to taste before adding it to the ice cream; 1 cup fruit purée is sufficient for 1 quart ice cream. Strawberry and raspberry purées are good additions as well as sweetened and puréed cranberries, coarsely chopped chestnuts from Whole Chestnuts in Vanilla Syrup (page 90) or even drained Prunes in Yunnan Tea and Armagnac (page 144).

2 cups milk
1 cup heavy cream
1 vanilla bean, split lengthwise
8 large egg yolks
½ cup sugar

In a saucepan scald the milk and the cream with the vanilla bean. Remove the pan from the heat and let the mixture stand, covered, for 15 to 20 minutes.

Beat the yolks with the sugar in a bowl until the mixture is thick and very pale. Remove the vanilla bean from the milk mixture and slowly whisk the milk mixture into the yolk mixture. Return the mixture to the pan and cook it over low heat, stirring frequently with a wooden spoon, until the custard thickens and coats the back of the spoon. Transfer the custard to a metal bowl set over a bed of ice and chill it, stirring occasionally to prevent a skin from forming.

Transfer the custard to an ice cream machine and freeze it according to the manufacturer's instructions.

Makes 1 quart

Overleaf: Cotton lavendar and Roman camomile in the Model Herb Garden at the Royal Horticultural Gardens, Wisley, Surrey.

BIBLIOGRAPHY

TECHNIQUES AND INGREDIENTS

Cameron-Smith, Marye — *The Complete Book of Preserving* London: Marshall Cavendish Limited, 1976

Hertzberg, Ruth; Vaughan, Beatrice; Greene, Janet — *Putting Food By* New York, Bantam Books, 1979

Hume, Rosemary; and Downes, Muriel — *The Cordon Bleu Book of Jams, Preserves and Pickles* London: Pan Books, 1977

Mabey, David — *In Search of Food* London: MacDonald and Janes, 1978

Mathiot, Ginette — *Je Sais Faire les Conserves* Paris: Editions Albin Michel, 1948

Nichols, Nell B.; and Larson, Kathryn — *Farm Journal's Freezing and Canning Cook Book* New York: Doubleday and Company, Inc., 1978

Pellaprat, H.P. — *Comment Faire ses Conserves* Paris: Flammarion, 1938

Stobart, Tom — *The Cook's Encyclopedia* London: Batsford Ltd., 1980

Stobart, Tom — *Herbs, Spices and Flavourings* London: The International Wine & Food Publishing Company, 1970

Time-Life Books — *The Good Cook: Preserving* London: Time-Life Books, 1980

CULINARY

Ali-Bab — *Gastronomie Practique* Paris: Flammarion, 1975

Aylett, Mary — *Country Fare* London: Odhams Press Ltd., 1956

Beeton, Isabella — *The Book of Household Management* London: Jonathan Cape, 1968

Bettelli, Enza Candela — *Un Amour de Confiture* Paris: Gentleman Editeur, 1987

David, Elizabeth — *Spices, Salt and Aromatics in the English Kitchen* London: Penguin, 1970

Grigson, Jane — *Jane Grigson's Fruit Book* London: Michael Joseph, 1982

Grigson, Jane — *Jane Grigson's Good Things in England* London: Michael Joseph, 1971

Hartley, Dorothy — *Food in England* London: MacDonald, 1954

Hutchinson, Peggy — *Peggy Hutchinson's Preserving Secrets* London: W. Foulsham & Co. Ltd., circa 1930

La Mazille — *La Bonne Cuisine du Périgord* Paris: Flammarion, 1947

Mabey, David; and Collison, David — *The Perfect Pickle Book* London: BBC Books, 1988

Reboul, J.B. — *La Cuisinière Provençale,* 6th edition Marseilles: Tacussell, 1985

Saint-Ange, E. — *Le Livre de Cuisine de Madame Saint-Ange* Paris: Larousse, 1927

White, Florence

Good Things
London: The Cookery
Book Club, 1971

HORTICULTURAL

Campbell, Susan

A Gardener's Lore
London: Century, 1983

Hibberd, Shirley

*The Amateur's Kitchen
Garden*
London: W.H. and
L. Collingridge, 1893

Lindley, George

*A Guide to the Orchard and
Kitchen Garden*
London: Longman,
Rees Orme, Brown, and
Green, 1831

Phillips, Henry

F.H.S. History of Fruits
London: Henry Colburn
and Co., 1823

Roach, F.A.

*Cultivated Fruits of
Britain: Their Origin and
History*
Oxford: Basil Blackwell,
1985

Scott-James, Helen

The Cottage Garden
Middlesex, England:
Penguin Books, 1987

ACKNOWLEDGMENTS

Many kind people have helped to make this book possible. My deepest appreciation goes to Leslie Stoker at Stewart, Tabori & Chang in New York, who remained eager from the start and patient to the end in the creation of this book. Also at Stewart, Tabori & Chang, I would like to thank Margaret Orto and Carolyn Petter for their enthusiasm and friendship. I am grateful to Lorraine Alexander for her meticulous editing, Elizabeth Woodson for her sensitivity to the layout and design, and to Kate Slate for seeing the project through with great good sense and patience.

In England, I am indebted to Susan Campbell for her advice, companionship on garden visits, and peaceful home in London; and to her son William, who deserves a medal for all his critical taste-testing and interest in the project.

I traveled extensively throughout England searching for suitable kitchen gardens to be photographed and was deeply touched by the warm reception and help by the following private home owners:

Mr. C. F. Hughesdon of Dunsborough Park Estate, Ripley, Surrey; and Derek Duffy, head gardener.

Mr. and Mrs. Stone of Little Mynthhurst Farm, Horley, Surrey; and David and Cynthia Forsyth, head gardeners.

The Jacobs family at Maabs, Stonegate, East Sussex.

Sabine de Mirbeck, l'Ecole de Cuisine Française, Litlington, Sussex; and Cristophe Buey, head chef.

Mr. and Mrs. Richard Mann of Litlington Place, Litlington, Sussex.

Richard Cotter of Benenden Walled Garden, Cranbrook, Kent.

Christine and John Harrison of North Court Shorewell, Isle of Wight.

Felicity and Richard Dick of Bayfield, Totland Bay, Isle of Wight.

Sir Michael and Lady Hanham of Deans Court, Wimborne, Dorset.

Major David and Lady Anne Rasch of Heale House, Salisbury, Wiltshire.

Mrs. Diane Saunders of Easton Grey House, Malmesbury, Wiltshire.

Mrs. Rosemary Verey of Barnsley House, Barnsley, Gloucestershire.

Lord and Lady Vestey of Stowell Park, Northleach, Gloucestershire.

Vicky and Peter Hingston of Old Kyrewood, Tenbury Wells, Worcester.

Mr. and Mrs. E. B. Walker of Hilltop, Martley, Worcester.

Patricia and John Hegarty of Hope End, Ledbury, Hereford.

The Murphys, Leeds, Yorkshire.

Rosemarie Gray of Eggleston Hall, Barnard Castle, Durham.

Mr. Henley, Isle of Wight Horticultural Society.

Mr. John Dupays, Hunstrete House Hotel, Chelwood, Avon.

The Tullburg family, Wiltshire Tracklements, Sherston, Wiltshire.

The Haunch of Venison, Salisbury, Wiltshire.

Mr. Head, Norfolk Lavender, Heacham, Norfolk.

Kings Bakery, Ripon, North Yorkshire.

Mr. P. MacMillan Browse, The Royal Horticultural Society, Woking, Surrey.

Jeremy and Sandra Trehane, James Trehane & Sons, Blueberry Orchards, Wimborne, Dorset.

Also in England, I would like to thank food stylist Louise Pickford for eagerly assisting and coordinating many photographic sessions with prop stylist Andrea Lampton; Judith Nunney and Jenny Taylor at Butlers Wharf Limited, for their extracurricular typing assistance; Paul Delfavero, chef and co-owner of the Blueprint Cafe in London, for his energy in preparing food for photography and for his supporting shoulder during the development of this book.

Finally, I would like to thank Richard Olney for being Richard and for sharing so much of his good sense about life, wine, and food, which will always remain an integral part of my life.

INDEX

Numbers in *italic* indicate photographs.

A

251

Designed by Elizabeth Woodson

Composed in Caslon 540 by
Graphic Arts Composition, Inc.,
Philadelphia, Pennsylvania.

Printed and bound by
Toppan Printing Company, Ltd.,
Tokyo, Japan.